Valkyries, selectors of heroes: their roles within Viking & Anglo Saxon Heathen beliefs.

Valkyries, selectors of heroes: their roles within Viking & Anglo Saxon Heathen beliefs.

By Pete Jennings

Brűnhild by Arthur Rackham

Gruff Books © 2016

Halstead, Essex UK.

Chapter Contents

Cover picture The Valkyries by Arthur Rackham (1867-1939)

Chapter 1. Definitions. Who or what are Valkyries?

Definitions and etymology

Are Valkyries bloodthirsty harpies or the rewarders of heroes? The simplest of questions sometimes lead to the most complex of answers, and I do not believe that I am being particularly abstruse by declaring that Valkyries cover a wide and sometimes contradictory range of ideas to different people. The general publics' often sole associated idea is that of 'The Ride of the Valkyries' by Wagner being a thrilling piece of classical music that even those with other musical tastes are able to recognise. Yet to get to the roots of what inspired Wagner and so many other people since to use the immensely powerful imagery of these much misunderstood entities we have to go back at least 1500 years to their Germanic roots, maybe further.

There is quite a good modern basic definition here:

> **Valkyrie,** also spelled Walkyrie, Old Norse Valkyrja ("Chooser of the Slain"), in Norse mythology, any of a group of maidens who served the god Odin and were sent by him to the battlefields to choose the slain who were worthy of a place in Valhalla. These foreboders of war rode to the battlefield on horses, wearing helmets and shields; in some accounts, they flew through the air and sea. Some Valkyries had the power to cause the death of the warriors they did not favour; others, especially heroine Valkyries, guarded the lives and ships of those dear to them. Old Norse literature made references to purely supernatural Valkyries and also to human Valkyries with certain supernatural powers. Both types of beings were associated with fairness,

brightness, and gold, as well as bloodshed.
(Encyclopædia Britannica, 2015)

There are a few alternative Old Norse names: In the poem Oddrúnargrátr [1] the term óskmey means 'wish maid.' One of the eke names (alternative nicknames denoting a particular quality) of Odin is Óski which means something like 'wish fulfilment' so the óskmey name may well link into that. In Nafnaþulur[2] a phrase 'Óðins meyjar' means Odin's maids, so is also thought to be another Old Norse kenning (metaphoric expression) for Valkyries. Other terms include Skjaldmeyjar (shield maidens) Valmeyjar (battle maidens), Hjalmmeyjar (helm maidens) and in their connected swan maiden role as Svanmeyja.

The Walkyrie, wælcyrge and wælcyrie spelling is used within Old English texts. There is debate as to whether the word was taken as a Viking import or formed from similar Old Germanic roots. The Old Norse version valkyrja (plural valkyrjur) originates from two component words: valr refers to the slain, kjósa means to choose. Thus it becomes 'chooser of the slain.'

Competing images

Although mentioned only about twelve times in surviving Old English texts, wælcyrie shows that the Anglo Saxons shared a similar belief in Valkyries to the Norse peoples, not surprising considering their shared Germanic origins. It does not mean that they necessarily pictured or believed in them in exactly the same way; there was no over-arching authoritive figure or text within the Heathen spiritual paths to impose a rigid theology, which could vary from village to village as well as country to country and time to time. Some writers seem to assume that because the two cultures feature similar gods and goddesses (albeit of slightly altered names) that their understanding of them was the same. There seems no proof of that.

What may be more relevant is the fact that Iceland partly converted late to Christianity in 1000 CE which gave it more chance to develop beliefs and mythology than other countries (such as England) which had achieved at least nominal conversion almost four centuries earlier in the mid - 7th century. Inevitably the nature of those who were literate tended to be Christian monks who were unlikely to write in detail about Heathen matters other than to condemn them. Even the information recorded in Iceland tended to be written down a couple of centuries after Christianisation by the likes of Snorri Sturlusson, but at least he did have earlier oral and written materials to draw upon. The quantity of data about Heathen beliefs and practices from Iceland outweighs that of other Scandinavian countries or England somewhat, so tends to have an undue influence upon what we think went on elsewhere. However, we can thank some English monks such as Bede for recording some native Heathen practices and beliefs.

Given that incoming religions tend to demonise their predecessors it is not surprising to find the term wælcyrige rapidly becoming associated with the character of a witch in Old English, something very different to its original concept. The first known usage of the modernised term Valkyrie was in 1770 according to the Meriam Webster Encyclopaedia.

Inevitably there is further confusion about the nature of Valkyries: Skuld, one of the Norns (Old Norse weavers of fate and destiny equivalent to the Old English Wyrd Sisters) was said to be a Valkyrie. There appear to be some that are demi-goddesses purely of the supernatural world, as assistants to the goddess Freyja, whilst at other times mortal women are given the same role.

Some scholars including Mortimer[3] have also suggested the Valkyries are synonymous with the Disir, ancestral female tutelary sprits that are distinctly separate to the two main families of deities, the Aesir and the Vanir. In Guðrúnarkviða 19 of the Poetic Edda,[4] the term Herjans dísir (Odin's disir) are used to describe them. Jacob Grimm[5] was clear in his researches that although he believed that Disir could be both a Norn and a Valkyrie, that the functions were distinct from each other and that the Norns were never described as riding as the Valkyries were. MacLeod and Mees[6] feel that the roles became confused and entangled later, not helped by relatively modern poets describing them without the benefit of knowing the complete mythology.

Jakob Grimm investigated whether there was a link between the Idis (Old English, plural Idisi) and the goddess Idunn, more usually known for her supply of magical apples.

In Beowulf[7] the mother of the monster Grendel is said to be an ides

> 1258: *Grendles modor*
> 1259: *ides, aglæcwif*

This would be an odd identity for the ferocious opponent of Beowulf to have if one goes with the usual straight translation of ides from the Old English as 'well-respected and dignified woman', connecting it with similar terms the Old Saxon Idis and Old High German it is.

Hilda Ellis Davidson[8] was of the opinion that some real life Heathen priestesses, present at rites for war (or killing of captives afterwards) may be the model of some Valkyries and further refers us to the story that the Arab diplomat Ibn Fadln; he wrote of his time amongst the Swedish Rus tribe in Russia when an old woman ritually executed a slave girl to accompany her dead master into the afterlife.

Then there are human females declared to be Valkyries: often the daughters of important men and possibly priestesses within the Heathen religion. Given that the leader of the Valkyries is said to be the Goddess Freyja it may well be that they are associated with her cult, but they could conceivably be dedicated to Odin / Woden as the war god (who supplanted Tyr / Tiwaz.) Given the plurality of beliefs and well recorded practice of having two or three deities represented on an altar they may have been involved with more than one god or goddess. E.g. Adam of Bremen[9] describes an altar with three idols at the main Swedish temple at Uppsala[10]. Valkyries may also have parallels (though not necessarily connections) with the Celtic goddess Morrígan.

Stephen Pollington[11] points out that the Queen of Hrothgar, the lady Wealhþeow who distributes mead to Beowulf[12] and his warriors has a symbology within her name: revised translation of this equates it to 'wæl þeow' i.e. servant of the slain, indicating this queen is of the formidable category wælcyrigean. He goes on to explore the name of the goddess Nanna, who mourns the loss of her husband Baldur: the plural nŏnnur is used in the Voluspá to mean female dependents, which in the context are Valkyries. He believes that her name is probably derived from the term nenþo which means powerful.[13] There is the further complication in which they are conflated with the Swan-Maidens myths

Simek[14] is of the opinion that Valkyries were originally demons of the dead whose interpretation altered to more humanised choosers of the slain who could fall in love with warriors when the concept of Valhall / Valhalla and Ásgarðr changed from a battlefield to a warrior paradise. Ásgarðr simply means the 'enclosure of the Aesir' in Old Norse. Valhalla is one hall within it, but many other are mentioned.[15] The battlefield for the final battle of Ragnarok is Vígríðr which means 'battle shaker plain' a place that is described as 100 miles wide in each direction.

According to Gylfaginning (in the Prose Edda) at Ragnarök the gods and their warriors will face the jötunn (giants), Loki, Hel, Surtr and their followers plus Fenrir the giant wolf and Jörmungandr the huge serpent. Odin will fight Fenrir, Thor fights Jörmungandr, Frey faces Surtr and Tyr the hell hound Garmr. Heimdallr who sounds the battle horn to summon the army and fights Loki. All are killed and Surtr's fiery sword burns the world except the handful of survivors saved to regenerate it.

In his translation of the Poetic Edda, Bellows[16] suggests that the concept of a supernatural warrior maiden was an early import into Scandinavia from South Germanic sources. Whatever they are, we are left with no distinct creation story for Valkyries, or even what their role is in Ragnarok, the final battle of the competing forces of the Norse mythology. Were they like the Norns apart from it, on some higher level or did they disappear because their job was done in supplying the best warriors for the final battle? Whilst before Ragnarok they could promise a warrior a form of heaven, the event itself only offers eternal death for most of its' participants with the exception of a handful of specified beings left to re-populate the worlds.[17]

We are not told what eventually happens to the Valkyries after Ragnarok in the stories that have survived. Since they are not listed with the named survivors one could envisage them having perished.

I do not buy into the wholesale assumption that Norse Valkyries = Celtic Morrígan = Classical Furies etc. Whilst they may have had an influence on each other, different cultures are capable of generating independent mythologies without the need to borrow from others. From the brief descriptions below it can be demonstrated that they are quite different in form to Valkyries:

The goddess of death Mórrígan (great queen) is from Irish mythology and mainly operates by herself upon the battlefield, sometimes in the form of a crow or alternatively a wolf or cow. However she does sometimes appear as part of a trio: Badb, Macha and Anand. The last of these is an alternative naming of Mórrígan.

The Furies are from the Greek mythology where they are also known as the Erinyes. In Roman mythology their equivalents are the Dirae. They are more goddesses of vengeance rather than being associated directly with death, punishing oath breakers and young people disrespectful to their elders. The Erinyes are crone like and having animalistic features such as snake hair. Sometimes they carry brass studded scourges to torment their victims.

The Valkyrie Role
Let me dispel one popular misconception: I have yet to read a credible text in which a Valkyrie actually fights. That may go against some firmly adopted modern ideas of warrior women and strong female heroines so sorry if I disappoint you.
They are certainly credited with being present at battles, encouraging male heroic behaviour and choosing the best. They may even fall in love with one and protect or destroy

them. Occasionally they may be described as bearing a spear or other weapon, or bearing a shield to protect someone.

They can fly through air or water, usually riding horses or sometimes wolves or boars. Although Victorian artists may have portrayed them as beautiful maidens they are more authentically described as frighteningly fierce, blood soaked and screaming. They may appear in a more peaceful guise as bearers of mead and food to the warriors in Valhalla. E.g. Hild, Thrud, and Hløkk are said to dispense ale in Valhalla, according to Grímnismál (Sayings of Grímnir)[18]

Three ale bearing Valkyries by Lorenz Frølich (1895)

The Danish writer Saxo Grammaticus[19] describes Hotherus finding 'woodland maidens' who already know his name and tell him that they decide the outcomes of battles and supported friends within it. They seem by their descriptions to be Valkyries despite Saxo not knowing their proper name. Saxo also wrote some lurid and exciting tales about a woman called Ladgerda fighting in battles, but most scholarly opinion deems them to be re-workings of earlier myths from other cultures.

Saxo also says that Valkyries feed Balder a special food to keep him from harm. In that version of the story (very different from the one more commonly known) his brother Hodr kills him with a magic sword that he had stolen from Mimingus. More usually Hodr is said to be blind and is tricked by Loki into killing Baldr by throwing a mistletoe dart at him.[20] Mistletoe had been missed out when all the plants and animals were asked to promise not to hurt Baldr by his mother Frigga.

Valkyries are also credited with being a part of the Wild Hunt of Odin / Woden, descending from winter gales to collect souls of the lost and unwary. (See my book *The Wild Hunt & its followers* for the full story.)[21]

In some stories Valkyries appear to have access to magic: one of their reputed leaders Freyja was the mistress of the Norse Seidr magic, which is particularly associated with women, although not exclusively. Odin is taught Seidr by Freyja, but is also a master of runes and Galdr magic. From some verses concerning Valkyrie magic it appears that some of their spells are similar to those associated with certain runes e.g. putting on or releasing war fetters. In others they appear to act like the Norns Urd, Verdandi & Skuld in weaving fate and destroying it. Urd approximately translates as 'fate or wyrd', Verdandi as 'necessity' and Skuld as 'being.' Do not be misled by erroneous texts that describe them as 'past, present and future.' There are subtle differences.

Norns Vanish by Arthur Rackham

Let's examine some descriptive evidence of Valkyries in an Old Norse text: it is a translation of a poem about the death of Brian Boru after his armies' victory over the Vikings at the Battle of Clontarf, Ireland in 1014:

Darraðarljóð (Spear Lay) from Njáls Saga[22]

> *Blood rains from the cloudy web*
> *On the broad loom of slaughter.*
> *The web of man grey as armour*
> *Is now being woven; the Valkyries*
> *Will cross it with a crimson weft.*
>
> *The warp is made of human entrails;*
> *Human heads are used as heddle-weights;*

The heddle rods are blood-wet spears;
The shafts are iron-bound and arrows are the
shuttles.
With swords we will weave this web of battle.

The Valkyries go weaving with drawn swords,
Hild and Hjorthrimul, Sanngrid and Svipul.
Spears will shatter shields will splinter,
Swords will gnaw like wolves through armour.

Let us now wind the web of war
Which the young king once waged.
Let us advance and wade through the ranks,
Where friends of ours are exchanging blows.

Let us now wind the web of war
And then follow the king to battle
Gunn and Gondul can see there
The blood-spattered shields that guarded the king.

Let us now wind the web of war
Where the warrior banners are forging forward
Let his life not be taken;
Only the Valkyries can choose the slain.

Lands will be ruled by new peoples
Who once inhabited outlying headlands.
We pronounce a great king destined to die;
Now an earl is felled by spears.

The men of Ireland will suffer a grief
That will never grow old in the minds of men.
The web is now woven and the battlefield reddened;
The news of disaster will spread through lands.

It is horrible now to look around
As a blood-red cloud darkens the sky.
The heavens are stained with the blood of men,
As the Valkyries sing their song.

We sang well victory songs
For the young king; hail to our singing!
Let him who listens to our Valkyrie song
Learn it well and tell it to others.

Let us ride our horses hard on bare backs,
With swords unsheathed away from here!

And then they tore the woven cloth from the loom
and ripped it to pieces,
Each keeping the shred she held in her hands.
The women mounted their horses and rode away,
Six to the south and six to the north.

This motif of weaving destinies with a horrific loom is one that we shall return to, and makes a link between Valkyries and Norns. Note also the words '*Only the Valkyries can choose the slain*' indicating it is their decision and not Odin's or Freyja's. Apart from the physical descriptions it can also be seen that they '*sing their song.*'

Swan Maidens

Some Valkyries appear as swan maidens, with associated feathered clothing. The Goddess Freyja is said to have a cloak of falcon feathers to enable her to fly, which she sometimes lends to others within the mythology. The swan maidens themselves are said to sometimes take off their swan clothes, and that forms the starting point for one of the great Germanic myths of the Poetic Edda, Völundarkviða.

Swan maidens by Arthur Rackham

Three swan maidens (the daughters of King Hlǫ́ðver or Hlaðgunn and King Kjárr) shed their clothes to swim in the river Rhine, and are spotted by three brothers who see them naked and hide their clothes, which sounds like the start of an American college comedy! They eventually consent to live as the wives of the three brothers for 7 years. One is Völundr, (also known as Wayland Smith) who learns how to be the world's greatest metal smith from his bride Ölrún (alternatively Alrun) with whom he has a son Heime. She leaves him with a ring when she eventually departs, from which he makes seven hundred copies. He also becomes a leader of the elves under the god Frey and survives an ordeal at the hands of the evil King Nidud.

Völundr's brothers Egil and Slagfiðr marry Hervor Alvít and Hlaðguðr Svanhvít (which possibly translates as 'swan white weaver of battles.) Egil becomes a notable archer and goes wandering when his wife departs, as does Slagfiðr.

Valkyries – Arthur Rackham

Depictions of Freyja

Chapter 2 Freyja & Odin: two leaders and more than two halls.

Freyja and Sessrumnir

Whilst she is well known and popular amongst the deities, there isn't a huge amount of source information concerning Freyja. Nasstrom[23] compiled a comprehensive document on sources and their details. Her name translates as 'Lady' just as her brother/ husband Frey's name translates as 'Lord.' She is said to ride in a cart pulled by cats (a challenging animal to harness and direct!) or even to ride a Siberian tiger. This is illustrated in the Schleswiger Dom[24], although there is no absolute proof that the figure is meant to be Freyja, it is generally believed to be so. Confusingly Freyja is also said to ride a magic battle boar called Hildisvín (battle-swine.) She also has a cloak of falcon feathers to enable her to fly, which she sometimes lends to other gods.

Frey and Freyja are the children of Njordr and members of the Vanir family of gods and are both concerned with fertility. In Freyja this is extended to lust, and she has the reputation of taking many lovers including Odin. Freyja even spends a night with each of four dwarves to gain the magical Brisingamen necklace. As a Vanir goddess she appears to be above the level of the Valkyries herself, who she is credited with leading.

As a Vanir goddess it seems that she was partnered in an incestuous marriage with her brother Frey, but once she lives with the Aesir Freyja is said to have a husband called Óðr but he is long lost, resulting in one of her titles being Þrungva (Lamenting for lost love) and amber is said to come from her tears. There has been inevitable debate as to whether Óðr is the same as Óðin / Woden; their names are similar and both are partners to Freyja. However, Sturlusson deals with them separately in the Poetic Edda, and credit Óðr as being the father of a daughter Hnoss (treasure, jewel) with Freyja, whereas no child is given for the Óðin / Freyja partnership.

Balder is fathered by Óðin on Frigg, (Frîja Old Germanic) his regular wife who in some sources is conflated (or confused) with Freyja. I am firmly of the personal opinion that Frigg & Freyja are two distinctly separate entities, as are Óðr and Óðin.

There was an interesting exchange of views on the Patheos website[25] in 2011; an individual identified as 'wyrddesigns' suggested that the main reason why Freyja is portrayed as being connected with Valkyries is because one of her titles in Njal's Saga is Valfreya which has been interpreted as 'Mistress of the Slain', but as she points out Odin has a title of Valfadir, yet no one tries to call him a Valkyrie. She translates the Valfreya title as 'Lady of the battle dead.' Freyja is credited with taking half of the heroes selected by the valkyries to Fólkvangr ('warrior fields') and her own Sessrumnir Hall (many seated.) This would fit in with Freyja's role without needing her to supervise Valkyries or choose the best fighters. This role of receiving half the warrior heroes is confirmed in both Gylfaginning and Skaldskaparmal which are both parts of the Prose Edda.

Another one of her titles in the Skaldskaparmal is Eidandi Valfalls which can be translated as 'possessor of the slain' which does not include choosing them on the battlefield. Having said that, on balance another one of her names is Skjálf (Shield) which does have a marshal quality to it but that could just refer to her general protective role. Freyja is said to pour ale at feasts in Skaldskarpamal and has other titles including Gefn (giving), Vanadís (goddess of the Vanir) and Sýr (Sow - a universal symbol of fecundity.)

There do seem to be some place names suggesting a dedication to a Freyja cult in both Sweden and Norway.[26]

Odin and Valhalla.

As can be deduced from above, Odin the chief god known as the Allfather gets the other half of the chosen dead warriors, (sometimes termed einherjar – 'those who fight alone') to feast in his hall of Glaðsheimr in Asgard each night and fight each other every day on the Battle Plain of Valhalla ('hall of the slain.') They enter the hall via a gate known as Valgrind that has sentinels of a wolf and eagle. The warrior spirits are miraculously cured from their wounds each night and eat meat from a daily revived boar called Sæhrímnir, cooked in a giant cauldron Eldhrímnir by the cook Andrímnir.[27] Glaðsheimr is said to be roofed with spears and full of weapons and armour. The Valkyries serve them an unending supply of mead flowing from the udders of the goat Heiðrun. One presumes that the possible hangover does not affect their fighting abilities the following day!

The aim is to have a formidable well practised army of warriors to fight on behalf of Odin at the final battle of Ragnarok, the Twilight of the Gods in which the forces of good and evil finally confront each other. Most combatants (human and supernatural) are wiped out with just a few survivors to restart the world anew. Interestingly no mention is made of the Valkyries in that story, maybe because their job is done. The story says that the armies will march out of 540 gates, each 800 warriors strong. That equates to 432,000, a number so large as to have been beyond the understanding or concept of the average person at the time in the way that infinity works now. Their enemies include the renegade god Loki, the fiery Surt, the monstrous Fenris Wolf and the world serpent Jormungand.

Mime and the Wanderer (Odin in disguise) by Arthur Rackham

Odin / Woden (which seem to be rooted in words meaning frenzy or fury) has about two hundred eke names (nicknames) reflecting the many attributes and roles he plays. E.g. Old Norse Grimr is his hooded form, and has given rise to several English place names containing references to it such as Grimsby, Lincolnshire, Grimes Graves in Norfolk and Grimspound on Dartmoor. The direct Old Norse term Odin survives in places such as Odin Mine, Derbyshire.

However, there are some place names directly related to his Old English name Woden such as Wednesbury, West Midlands (ex Wodensbury – Woden's Burgh) Wednesfield, West Midlands (Woden's Field) Wanstead, Essex (Woden's Stead) and Wambrook, Somerset. (Woden's Brook.) There are far fewer place names associated with Odin in Scandinavia than the seemingly more popular gods such as Thor. Woden is the traditional leader of the Wild Hunt in England, which is a pan – European belief in a troop of mounted spirits searching for lost souls, mainly across winter night skies.)[28] He is said to be accompanied by various historic figures as well as the Valkyries.

Odin seems to be constantly on the search for knowledge in the mythology. He gives an eye in exchange for knowledge from Mimir's Well and hangs for nine days and nights, (wounded by his own spear Gugnir) from the world tree Yggdrassil to gain the knowledge of the runes. He raises a dead witch Groa to question her and has two ravens Huginn (thought) and Muninn (memory) which fly around the world to report back to him on his high seat above the worlds. He gains knowledge of Seidr magic from Freyja and steals the mead of poetry and eloquence to bring back to his followers. He also has two pet wolves Freki & Geri (Greedyguts & Gobbler) and an eight legged horse called Sleipnir. He sometimes walks the world disguised with a broad brimmed hat concealing his lost eye and a large cloak.

Raging Wotan by Arthur Rackham

On some memorial stones showing Odin the Valknut symbol is used. This design of three interlocking triangles does not appear with any other entity, so may be associated with him. I personally wonder whether the points symbolise the nine interlocking worlds of Yggdrassil. However, Eirik Westcoat argues that the Valknut represents the idealised heart of a hero.[29]

Three and nine are the main two magical numbers associated with the Norse mythology, rather than the seven or thirteen of many other cultures. Odin's ring Draupnir drips eight more rings every nine nights.

Other places of the dead.
As Diana Paxon[30] and many others point out, there are many other options for the spirits of the dead to go to excluding Glaðsheimr in Asgard or Sessrumnir Hall in Fólkvangr. There is for a start Hel, where Balder finishes up. Initially it is described as a good place (after all Balder is the purest of gods) and it is only after Christianisation that it gets negative associations. There is however one bad place in the realm of Hel called Nastrond for where oath breakers, murderers and adulterers are destined. Other halls for the dead include Bilskrnir ('lightning') belonging to Thor / Thunor but I wouldn't expect it to be suitable for those seeking a quiet life!

Odin's wife Frigga has Fensilar ('fenlands') and Balder has Breiðblikk ('broad view'.) Forseti the god of justice conducts trials in Glitnir, the 'Hall of Splendour' and the ever watchful Heimdall has Himminbjorg. ('Heaven Hall.') Saga tells stories in Sokkvabekk ('sunken benches'), Ydalir is the home of Ullr and it means something like 'Yew Dale.' Since Ullr is an archer, having yew to make the best bows with would seem appropriate. The hall of Vidar is Landvidi (possibly 'White Land'.)

Thor by Arthur Rackham

The goddess Skadi is situated away from Asgard in the mountains of Jotunheim, the home of the giants and is called Thrymheim, the 'thunder home.' The sea god Noatun and his wife Ran also have their home away from Asgard in the harbour by the sea known as Noatun. ('Shipyard') in Vanaheim the land of the Vanir deities.

The gods all have seats in Odin's Glaðsheimr (where Valaskjalf the hall of Vali is also situated) but the goddesses have their own hall Vingol.

Some heroes seem to stay within their grave mounds (sometimes venturing out) and In Iceland I have visited Helgafell. In the Eyrbyggja saga[31] a priest called Thorolf declares that the ancestors go into this hill, and one must wash before climbing it and not urinate on it. Thoughtfully the Icelandic authorities provide wash basins and a loo at the base of it!

Helgafell, Iceland.

Chapter 3 Individual names, meanings and their sources

On all sides saw I, Valkyries assemble,
Ready to ride, to the ranks of the gods;
Skuld bore the shield, and Skogul rode next,
Guth, Hild, Gondul, and Geirskogul.
Of Herjan's[32] maidens the list have ye heard,
Valkyries ready to ride o'er the earth.

(Völuspá v31)

It is generally thought that some historic writers invented some Valkyrie names to emphasise or pad out a part of the story they were telling. There are also some Valkyrie names that seem very similar and may be variants of a single name. Nevertheless I have decided to compile a chart of those names (using the most popular spellings) that I have found within my researches, together with a possible meaning and main source. There may be even more, so I do not claim this as a complete list but as an ongoing work in progress. I have deliberately omitted any that I feel are later inventions or of doubtful origin, and some Valkyries are shown with their alternative names listed as well.

Valkyrie name	Possible meaning of name	Source(s) of name
Alvítr	All White	Völundarkviða in Poetic Edda
Biört	Bright	Fjölsvinnsmál in Poetic Edda
Brynhildr, Brűnhild	Byrnie of Battle or Bright Battle	Nibelungenlied (Daughter of King Budli according to Völsunga saga) Skáldskaparmál
Eir	Mercy	Fjölsvinnsmál in Poetic Edda + Nafnaþulur

Geirahöð	Battle of spears	Gylfaginning in the Prose Edda + Grímnismál
Geiravőr	Spear Vor	Nafnaþulur
Geirdriful	Spear Flinger	Nafnaþulur
Geironul	Charges with spear	Grímnismál + Nafnaþulur
Geirskogul	Spear Shaker	Darraðarljóð a poem quoted in Njal's saga + Hákonarmál, Völuspá, Nafnaþulur
Göll	Battle Cry	Grímnismál + Gylfaginning in the Prose Edda + Nafnaþulur
Göndul	Enchanted Stave	Darraðarljóð a poem quoted in Njal's saga + Völuspá, Nafnaþulur
Gudrun	Battle-rune	Volsunga Saga
Gunnr / Guðr	Battle / War	Darraðarljóð a poem quoted in Njal's saga + Völuspá Gylfaginning, Nafnaþulur, Skáldskaparmál
Gunwar/ Gunnvör/ Gunnora	War-Oath	Gylfaginning in the Prose Edda
Hedin	Heath dweller	Ragnarsdrápa
Herfjötur	War-Fetter	Grímnismál + Gylfaginning in the Prose Edda, Nafnaþulur
Herja	Devastate	Nafnaþulur in Prose Edda
Hervor Alvít / Alvítr	All White bringer of war	(Daughter of King Louis) Völundarkviða in Poetic Edda
Hild / Hildr / Hilda	Battle	Darraðarljóð (a poem quoted in Njal's saga) & Grímnismál + Gylfaginning in the Prose Edda & Ragnarsdrápa

Valkyries, selectors of heroes: their roles within Viking & Anglo Saxon Heathen beliefs.

		Völuspá, Nafnaþulur
Hjalmþrimul	Female Warrior	Nafnaþulur + Darraðarljóð
Hjörþrimul	Battle of Swords	Darraðarljóð a poem quoted in Njal's saga
Hlaðgunn Swanhwid/ Svanhvít	Swan white weaver of battles	(Daughter of King Louis) Völundarkviða
Hlökk	Din of Battle	Grímnismál + Gylfaginning in the Prose Edda, Nafnaþulur
Hrist	Shaker	Grímnismál + Gylfaginning in the Prose Edda, Nafnaþulur
Hrund	Pricker	Nafnaþulur
Kára	Wild	Helgakviða Hundingsbana II
Kreimhildr/ Grimhild/ Gudrun	Helm of Battle	(Wife of Sigurd, daughter of King Dancrat of Burgundy.) Volsunga saga + Thiðreks saga
Mist	Mist	Grímnismál + Gylfaginning in the Prose Edda, Nafnaþulur
Ölrún/ Alrun	Ale rune	(Daughter of King Kjárr of France) Völundarkviða
Ráðgríð	Counsel of Peace	Gylfaginning in the Prose Edda.
Randgrid/ Randgríðr/ Randgrith	Shield-truce	Gylfaginning in the Prose Edda. Grímnismál, Nafnaþulur
Reginleif	Power Truce	Grímnismál + Gylfaginning in the Prose Edda, Nafnaþulur
Róta	Turmoil	Gylfaginning in the Prose Edda
Sanngriðr	Very Cruel	Darraðarljóð a poem quoted in Njal's saga
Sigrdrífa	Victory Blizzard/ Urger	Sigrdrífumál

Valkyries, selectors of heroes: their roles within Viking & Anglo Saxon Heathen beliefs.

Sigrún	Victory Rune	(Daughter of King Hogni in Poetic Edda) Helgakviða Hundingsbana I &II + Volsunga Saga.
Skamöld	Sword Time	Nafnaþulur
Skeggjöld	War Axe / Age	Grímnismál + Gylfaginning in the Prose Edda, Nafnaþulur
Skogul	Shaker	Darraðarljóð a poem quoted in Njal's saga + Grímnismál + Gylfaginning in the Prose Edda. Hákonarmál, Völuspá, Nafnaþulur
Skuld	Becoming	(Also a Norn) Darraðarljóð a poem quoted in Njal's saga Völuspá, Gylfaginning, Nafnaþulur
Sólbiört	Sun-Bright	Úlfhams saga
Storm	Storm	Darraðarljóð a poem quoted in Njal's saga
Svanmeyja	Swan Maiden	Generic term?
Sváva	Sleep Maker	(Human daughter of king Eylimi according to Poetic Edda.) Helgakviða Hjörvarðssonar
Sveið	Noise	Nafnaþulur
Svipul	Changeable	Darraðarljóð a poem quoted in Njal's saga, Nafnaþulur
Swanhwid/ Svanvít	Swan-White	Völundarkviða
þögn	Silence	Nafnaþulur
þrima	Fight	Nafnaþulur
Þrúðr / Thruth	Power	Gylfaginning in the Prose Edda + Grímnismál, Nafnaþulur

Valkyries, selectors of heroes: their roles within Viking & Anglo Saxon Heathen beliefs.

Some individual Valkyrie stories.

Brynhild / Brynhildr/ Brűnhild

Brűnhild dazed by Arthur Rackham

Brűnhild chose to let the wrong king (Hjalmgunnar) die in a battle, so was penalised by Odin who insisted that she could only marry a mortal man. She reacted by holding out for a hero and placed her bed in a ring of fire. The hero Sigurd who had already killed the dragon Fafnir crosses it twice, but she is tricked into marrying Gunnar, the brother of one of her fellow Valkyries Gudrun. This means that Gudrun can marry Sigurd, but when he dies it is the sorrowful Brűnhild who joins him on the funeral pyre. The Volsunga Saga has the complete tale which also involves a magic ring, shape shifting and all sorts of deceptions. In its' Germanic form the Nibelungenlied is of course the inspiration for Wagner's Ring Cycle sequence of operas.

Svava
Whilst riding with eight other Valkyries Svava meets a warrior who has not yet been named. She calls him Helgi and they marry, but it is not explained why his parents Hiorvard and Sigrlinn had not named him after birth. His half - brother Hedin desires her and the two brothers duel. Her husband is mortally wounded and tells his wife to accept his brother Hedin as her lover but instead she kills herself. They are reborn as Sigrun and Helgi Sigmundsson. (See next story.)

Sigrun
This Valkyrie was the daughter of King Hogni, betrothed to Hodbrodd the son of King Gramr. She wanted the hero Helgi instead, and encouraged him to fight her unwanted suitor. Some old enemies of Helgi, the Hunding brothers become allies with Hodbrodd, but they are all killed by Helgi and his half- brother Sinfjotli. The main source of this story is Helgi Hundingsbani II. (See chapter 5)

Hljod
Hljod, the daughter of the giant Hrimnir is labelled an óskmær (wish maiden) in the Volsunga Saga. It is unusual to have giant progeny as Valkyries. However, the line between the gods and their enemies the Thurz giants are often blurred. Despite being often depicted as fighting giants with his hammer mjollnir, Thor receives the gift of magic gauntlets and a belt of strength from one and has sex with another. He himself is of half giant stock himself as the son of Odin and the giantess Jǫrð the earth goddess, so in attacking giants he may be symbolically be fighting a part of his own nature.

Hljod is summoned by Odin to give a magic fertility apple to Rerir who is having difficulty in having a child with his wife. It works but Rerir dies and his wife's pregnancy lasts six years.

She herself dies giving birth to the son Volsung, but he then grows very fast.

Hrimnir instructs his daughter to marry Volsung and they have a daughter and ten sons. The first of the babies are the twins Sigmund and Signy.

Folklore

There are some Scandinavian folk beliefs that dew falls from the manes of Valkyrie horses galloping across the sky, and that the northern lights or aurora borealis are where their trails cross it.

The Dises by Dorothy Hardy (1909)

Chapter 4. A Warrior based society and its implications

The phrase 'warrior based society' is sometimes repeated without reflecting upon what it means in real terms: in the modern world we do not have a direct comparison in the majority of (allegedly) civilised countries. Unless a person joins the military, the police or emergency services they will not usually have an opportunity to demonstrate warrior or hero - like qualities, and in most cases they will not expect that society prioritise their needs. Otherwise military budgets would be unlimited, as would the resources given to disabled war veterans, which clearly they are not.

The attitude of many Viking and Saxon Heathen warriors in believing a death on the battlefield was superior to that of dying in bed ('straw dead') of old age or illness may have lessened the effect of injured soldiers being reliant on society for support, but this issue must still have existed. Certainly professional warriors of that time seemed to have been given the best food, drink and choice of partners by written accounts, as well as land and spoils of war if they were successful.

One may also perceive that to attain Valhalla they would not only wish to be brave, but be seen to do so, as this short fragment by Icelander Skúli þorsteinsson demonstrates:

Valkyrie of the drink vessel
Won't have seen me in the rear
Of the regiment when I gave
Gory wounds for the dawn flier. (raven)

The poet survived on the victorious side in the Battle of Svold in 1000 E.[33]

It is true of course that today men and women do have the opportunity to be warriors in ways that do not directly involve combat; being an ecological protestor or an advocate for vulnerable people or animals. Being an opposition politician or writing to make political points under totalitarian regime; Opposing big business interests or challenging the power of authorities or the media giants. These are all fields in which people of today may become acknowledged as heroes and there are many more such as aid workers, carers, social workers, teachers, medical staff, youth leaders, community leaders etc. However, we do not have a warrior elite that take precedence over other sections of the community, so we are not a 'warrior based society.'

Unfortunately the term hero has been much debased in the same way that celebrity has. Participating in an activity such as sport or the arts or doing a job that one chooses does not make one a hero, yet it is often construed as such. It is only when they go beyond what is expected and make personal sacrifice to do it (injury, time, reputation, employment etc.) that they become a hero. Most heroes do get frightened but overcome it. A soldier with no fear is often considered by his comrades to be a liability. It should also be remembered that in building a person up to be regarded as a hero we may disregard that they may have 'feet of clay' and have the same human foibles, fears and inadequacies as everyone else.

In the Early Mediaeval period there were some professional soldiers: Kings, leaders, bodyguards and mercenary bands. The bulk of an army would be formed from men who had not chosen to specialise in fighting, and may have until shortly beforehand been farmworkers. They were unlikely to understand the politics and threats between kingdoms or be aware of where other places were, let alone what they were like, or whether they were worth trying to conquer or defend against. Other than wanting to protect their own family and small community they would not have had a strong motivation or ability for combat.

Part of a war band leader's job then would be to do some rapid training, armament, marching and enthusing these involuntary recruits to fight hard and not run away. It is possible that a religious appeal incorporating Valkyries could have been instrumental in that, in the same way that later Christian Crusaders or Islamic Jihadists are promised entry to heaven and its delights.

Pollington[34] comments that a warrior from a good family may even have a belief in a personal supernatural protector known as a fylgjukona or fylgja, meaning a 'following woman' who represented the good luck that his family had amassed by their deeds. Such an entity seems very similar, if not identical to a Valkyrie in the way it operates.

The role of women of women in a warrior based society.
Whilst the majority of women may have been fearful for the consequences of their loved ones going to war, inevitably there may have been some that encouraged or even instigated it. Whilst some women were deliberately married to a member of an opposing tribe as a way of encouraging peace (known sometimes as 'peace weavers') there are incidences when strong women encouraged their men to 'do the honourable thing' including fighting those who insulted or challenged them E.g. the un-named wife of King Raedwald of East Anglia is said to have urged him to extend hospitality and refuge to Edwin of Northumbria and reject the gifts of ambassadors sent by his usurper to hand him over. This eventually led to Raedwald fighting the Battle of the River Idle and returning Edwin to his throne. There are also several

incidences in the Icelandic sagas where women incite their men to violence.

The strong influence of women within Germanic society was noted by the Roman historian Tacitus,[35] with deference given to their intuition and prophetic powers. That is reflected several centuries later when the Norsemen settled in Greenland pay huge deference to a visiting 'Little Sybil' to their community who is there to give prophesy from a high seat.[36] It should also be remembered that women had far greater legal status before Christianisation, being able to divorce and hold property independently in many Heathen cultures.

However, women would pay heavily if their side were defeated: rape, slavery, death or being deprived of their husband, children, home, food or belongings. A warrior husband may have fought hard to have prevented this fate for his loved ones rather than for a belief in a cause, leader or country.

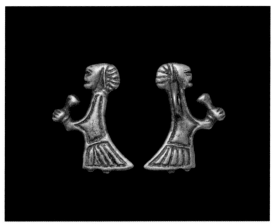

10th century pendant

Female warriors
Although it does not have been common, there are recorded examples of female warriors in Viking society. Clover[37] states

that based upon the Baugatal section of the Gragas law codes and information from Saxo Grammaticus[38] there were specific pre-conditions: a crime such as murder had been committed against her family, she had not been married and had not got any close male relatives that could receive weregild (legal damages) or act upon their behalf.

Whilst it has to be admitted Saxo Grammaticus is not totally reliable, Jochens[39] looks at the subject and my own researches for *Heathen Paths* [40] reveals at least several female individuals actively involved in combat: a pirate called Sela and Lathgertha who was said to be a skilled fighter. Jesch[41] highlights Hetha leading the right flank of Harald War-Tooth's army and Visna the standard bearer. There was Vebiorg who fought at Brávellir. Visna and Vebiorg died in battle, demonstrating their active roles. Rusila fought her brother Thrond for the throne of Norway and there is Alvid, another pirate leader and her daughter Gurith.

Shield Maidens
The term Shield Maiden (Old Norse skjaldmeyjar) is sometimes applied to Valkyries or human women. It does not seem to be a clearly defined term, but one could imagine a defensive role in the same way that some kings had a shield bearer to assist their defence. Certainly some Valkyries are credited with protecting their favoured hero, and in a similar way some human women have tried to protect their man.

> *Even a real shieldmaiden gets a mention in Ágrip Jökuldæla sögu. Unfortunately she chases swans until she bursts, while the hero of the story is busy duelling. (Hulda)*[42]

Figures from Tissø

The Gísla saga[43] includes details of two fighting women: Auður defends her husband against a band of armed attackers and Þórdís seizes the sword of her dead brother Gísli from his assassin and seriously wounds the man.

In the Laxdæla saga[44] a formerly married woman Auður puts on men's clothing to attack her ex-husband Thord who has been slandering her.

Blenda is the heroine of a Swedish legend (Blendasägnen) from Småland. She led her female comrades from Värend in an attack that apparently repulsed a Danish force.

At the Battle of Dunheidi, Hervőr, daughter of King Angantyre led an army against Hlőd and Humli, the sons of King Humli. She was heavily outnumbered and was killed, but impressed her opponents so much with her ferocity and skill that they buried her honourably in a mound.

Whilst no evidence of individual Saxon women warriors has survived, the Old English poem *Judith*[45] (possibly by Cynewulf or his students) features an Israelite sword fighting woman. It is based upon a book dropped from the Bible (part of the

Apocrypha) but turned into a homily by Ælfric of Eynsham, a tenth century abbot.[46] It was written at a time of Viking attacks and seems to exhort the Saxons to defend the country and fight them. Ironically it seems to take the same tone as the women described previously as encouraging their men to fight, being the conscience of the warrior and instructing them to 'do the right thing.'

Archaeological anomalies.
In recent years there has been debate between experts about some of the findings in Early Medieval period graves. In short, some sword- like items have been found within distinctly female burials. Although some may have been a family heirloom sword with no male heir to pass it on to, several have been identified as 'weaving swords.' These tend to be about half the average length of conventional swords at the time at around 17inches (45cm) and associated with a few Anglo Saxon and Germanic high status female graves of the late 6th and early 7th century.[47]

It is generally agreed that one can beat down the thread in weaving with a flat wooden beater, which begs the question "why have expensive metal ones?" In at least one case the metal beater has been made by recycling, shortening and converting an old sword which is fairly logical, but having heavy metal 'weaving swords' instead of lightweight wooden battens seems to be illogical and wasteful of the valuable resource of metal. Of course, it could be a flagrant display of wealth and status (a familiar theme in many Early Medieval activities) but the weight makes them less practical than their wooden or bone counterparts.

However, one must admit that they exist: an entry on the Museums of Scotland website shows an iron weaving sword from a Norse woman's grave at Westness on the island of Rousay in Orkney. She is believed to have died in childbirth between 850-900 CE. The socket at one end shows remains of a wooden handle. Other items connected with weaving were also found there along with some high quality materials.[48]

In the past, deciding the gender of a skeleton has often been based upon observing particular bones. A wide pelvis tends to indicate female, and heavy ridged brows a male. When those bones were absent, a deduction may be made from the accompanying grave goods. One cannot be over critical of archaeologists deciding that weapons indicated a man and jewellery a female for instance. However with new more sophisticated scientific methods at their disposal they have found that the reverse is sometimes the case: a man may have beads or a brooch, a woman a spearhead or shield boss. Some previously categorised skeletons are now being reviewed. It is possible (but not certain) that a female buried with weapons may possibly have been a warrior.

One has to consider a separate indication for weaving swords not being the same as combat swords: in most Anglo Saxon burials such as at Dover Buckland in Kent (burials 20, 38 & 48) weaving swords seem to have been laid in positions away from the area of the chatelaine holding other female utensils (and where a combat sword is usually deposited beside a male burial) i.e. against the left leg.[49] However there have been a couple of exceptions to that: Dover Buckland burial 250 and Edix Hill Barrington burial 18 both have the items beside the left leg, the same position as for a male burial with sword.

I would suggest a further possibility (without any research or proof) into the interpretation of sword like objects buried with females: a female buried with a weapon may have taken part in a ritual drama in which she portrayed a Valkyrie. We do know from illustrations on weapons, helmets etc. that ritual enactment of religious ideas seems to have been carried out with some of their other beliefs e.g. the spear dancers found on both Saxon and Viking artefacts. Wouldn't it make sense for this to happen with Valkyrie beliefs, especially in times of war? Let me make it clear: I am not saying that it did happen, only that there is the possibility that it may have done.

The extent of confusion is well documented and explored by Gardera[50] who examines the evidence of female graves containing remains of axes, spears etc. in Scandinavia. He says that it is not always possible to define a skeleton as a female warrior because of their presence: an axe may be for domestic use and there is a suggestion that some magical wands could have been in the form of spears.

Brünhild with horse by Arthur Rackham

Chapter 5 Literary Sources

Elder Poetic Edda

The sources of this collection[51] are Old Norse poems from Iceland and Greenland of varying dates, mainly collected together in the Codex Regius. There are references to Valkyries in the following sections: Grímnismál, Helgakviða Hjörvarðssonar, Helgakviða Hundingsbana I, Helgakviða Hundingsbana II, Sigrdrífumál, Völundarkviða, and Völuspá. There are several English translations of the texts which are not completely consistent with each other on names etc., and which may contain variations in the contents depending on the sources used.

Grímnismál

When Odin (disguised in his Grímnir form) is tortured by his host he is very thirsty and tells the young Agnar that he wishes that the Valkyries will bring him drink in a horn. He names them as Hrist, Mist; Skeggjöld, Skögul, Hildr, Þrúðr, Hlökk, Herfjötur, Göll, Geirahöð, Randgríð, Ráðgríð and Reginleif and adds that they all bear ale to the einherjar. I.e. the heroes that enter Asgard. Herfjötur is interesting in that her name means 'war fetter.' Given that elsewhere there are references to runic charms to put fetters on enemies or release them from yourself there is speculation as to whether this is a psychological weapon associated with Herfjötur rather than manacles: the ability to 'freeze' an opponent from action is taught in several martial arts, as how to resist it. Burfield[52] goes as far as to suggest the possibility that it could be the form of battlefield paralysis that goes with PTSD (Post Traumatic Stress Disorder.)

Helgakviða Hjörvarðssonar

The story is about an un-named young prince, who does not speak. He is the son of King Hjörvarðr of Norway and Sigrlinn of Sváfaland, and witnesses nine Valkyries going by while he is sitting on a burial mound. That point may be important, as the magical practice of utiseta i.e. sitting out as described in Heimskringla[53] and the Gulathingslog Norwegian law code.[54] The prince is attracted to one in particular who is Sváva, 'the bright faced' who is king Eylimi's daughter. He recognises her as having protected him in battles. She gives him the name Helgi, (holy one) and he is able to speak and asks for a naming gift (a common Norse custom.) saying that he will not receive it if he cannot have her as his wife. Sváva offers him a hoard of valuable swords at Sigarsholm, one of which is very special.

At one stage of the story a man called Atli has a verbal insult contest (flyting) with a female jötunn (giant) called Hrímgerðr. She reveals that she has seen twenty seven Valkyries around Helgi, led by a particularly fair one. (27 is a special combination magical number: 3 X 3 X 3). 3 & 9 are the most frequent magical numbers in Norse tales. One would only expect a hero to be attended by one Valkyrie, but presumably the other twenty six are following their leader Sváva. Hrímgerðr stays flyting until sunrise turns her to stone, a fate met by dwarves elsewhere.

> Three times nine girls, but one girl rode ahead,
> white-skinned under her helmet;
> the horses were trembling, from their manes
> dew fell into the deep valleys,
> hail in the high woods;
> good fortune comes to men from there;
> all that I saw was hateful to me

Once Helgi becomes King, he asks King Eylimi for his daughter Sváva in marriage. It is all agreed. Although they are very much in love, Sváva continues staying with her father the king whilst Helgi continues to go out raiding. The poem says that Sváva "was a Valkyrie just as before" confirming that this is a human female who doubles as a leader of Valkyries. After Helgi eventually succumbs to a war wound it is said that the couple are reincarnated. (See Helgakviða Hundingsbana I)

Helgakviða Hundingsbana I
The Norns arrive to foretell the fate of the new son of Sigmund (son of Volsung) and his wife Borghild in Brálund. When he reaches 15 years old this son Helgi Hundingsbane killed a man called Hunding. The sons of Hunding demanded wergild (financial compensation) but he refused and met them in battle. In it they were all killed. He encountered a Valkyrie woman called Sváva who complained that she was being married off to a man called Höðbroddr, the son of King Granmar against her will. Helgi says that he will fight on her behalf because Höðbroddr is not worthy enough to marry her. He gathers an army who march for the battle. He defeats Höðbroddr and takes Sváva as his own bride.

During the fight Valkyries are seen overhead by Helgi.

> Then light shone from Logafell,
> and from that radiance there came bolts of lightning;
> wearing helmets at Himingvani came the valkyries.
> Their byrnies were drenched in blood;
> and rays shone from their spears.

The Valkyries here are described as wearing helmets, mail coats being drenched in blood and with shining spears. They are seen by Helgi Hundingsbane over the battlefield of Logafjöll. The battle is still continuing and he asks them whether they will come with the warriors that night. When the battle finishes with Helgi victorious a Valkyrie called Sigrún tells him that she is betrothed (against her will) to Höðbroddr of the Hniflungs,

Helgi agrees to take on the Hniflungs on behalf of Sigrún. She then protects him.

Helmeted valkyries came down from the sky
the noise of spears grew loud, they protected the prince;
then said Sigrun, the wound-giving valkyries flew,
the troll-woman's mount was feasting on the fodder of ravens

Her mount in the poem is a wolf, rather than the more usual horse, and it eats the corpses (fodder of ravens) Ravens traditionally feed on the dead of battlefield. Ravens are also associated with Odin, who keeps two (Huggin and Munnin) as spies upon the world.

Helgakviða Hundingsbana II
King Sigmund (son of Völsung) and his wife Borghild (of Brálund) have a son named Helgi. He was named after Helgi Hjörvarðsson (see Helgakviða Hundingsbana I.) There is a suggestion that he may be a reincarnation of him. His tribe have a long running feud with the extensive Hunding family. Helgi adopts disguises to move amongst them and kills a son of the family called Hæmingr. He escapes and eventually faces the father King Hunding. He then acquires his second name Hundingsbana (the bane of the Hundings.)

After killing King Hunding he has to escape and ends up eating raw meat with his warriors at Brunarvagar which he has rustled to survive. He encounters Sigrún, daughter of King Högni and who is also a Valkyrie reincarnated from Sváva. (See part I.) She had been promised in marriage to

Hothbrodd, the son of king Granmarr by her father king Högne. After encouragement from Sigrún Helgi sails in a large fleet of ships for Frekastein but gets caught in a huge storm. Lightning strikes one ship and they think they are all doomed until they see nine Valkyries riding above them led by Sigrún.

From heaven there came, the maidens helmed,
The weapon clang grew, who watched over the king;
Spoke Sigrún fair, the wound givers flew,
And the horse of the giantess raven's-food had

'Wound givers' is believed to be another epithet for Valkyries. It appears that Sigrún is riding a wolf here, as a horse would not eat the dead 'ravens-food' warriors.

Helgi and his brother Sinfjötli won the battle against Granmarr and his sons and Helgi takes Sigrún as his wife with whom he had several sons. Later he dies at the hands of Sigrún's brother Dagr. Dagr is his brother in law, the brother of Sigrún. He had been on the opposing side but was spared because of then swearing allegiance to Helgi. However he had later sacrificed to Odin and been given a magical spear to kill Helgi with in revenge for the killing of his father and the rest of his family by Helgi. He does go to Sigrún and tells her what has happened. Sigrún lays a curse upon her brother Dagr for killing her husband. (See the curse from this story in chapter 7.)

Helgi is buried in a great mound, yet he is still able to spend a night with Sigrún there once when she visits it from Valhalla. When he does not return to it again, Sigrún dies of grief but they reincarnate again according to the lost text Káruljóð; the couple reincarnate yet again, Helgi as Helgi Haddingjaskaði and Sigrún as the Valkyrie Kára, daughter of Halfdan.

Incidentally the story has a phrase that translates as "fed the goslings of Gunn's sisters". Gunn's sister is Gunnr and a Valkyrie. It is thought that the goslings refer to ravens.

Sigrdrífumál

The male hero Sigurd is heading south towards the lands of the Franks; from the mountain Hindarfell he sees a light burning brightly up into the sky. On approaching he finds a Skjaldborg, which is a shield wall with a pennant flying over it. He penetrates the shield wall (in re-telling's sometimes a ring of flames) and finds a sleeping warrior in full armour. On removing the helmet he is surprised to find that it is a female. Her armour is so tight that it is embedded into her body, so he uses his sword to cut her out of it. She wakes up and they start talking to each other.

The woman, who is a Valkyrie called Sigdrifa gives Sigurd a horn of mead to help him to remember all that she tells him. She recites a Heathen prayer, one of few that survive intact today:

> Heill dagr!
> Heilir dags synir!
> Heil nótt ok nift!
> Óreiðum augum
> lítið okkr þinig
> ok gefið sitjöndum sigr!

> Heilir æsir!
> Heilar ásynjur!
> Heil sjá in fjölnýta fold!
> Mál ok mannvit
> gefið okkr mærum tveim
> ok læknishendr, meðan lifum.

This translates as

Hail, day!
Hail, sons of day!
And night and her daughter now!
Look on us here
with loving eyes,
That waiting we victory win.

Hail to the gods!
Ye goddesses, hail,
And all the generous earth!
Give to us wisdom
and goodly speech,
And healing hands, life-long.

Sigdrifa recites a prayer by Arthur Rackham

Sigdrifa explains to Sigurd that she once selected a King Hjalmgunnar to die in battle. The god Odin had promised him victory and so was very angry. He told her that she would never be allowed to be victorious in battle again and condemned her to marriage with a mortal. She responded by telling Odin that she had sworn to not wed any man that knew fear. Odin pricked her with a sleep thorn and she had slept since then.

Presumably by penetrating the mighty shield wall (instead of the ring of fire featured in some other stories) Sigurd had proved himself, because he asked Sigdrifa to share her knowledge of magic, prophesy and runes. She agreed. She tells him to carve 'victory runes' on the hilt of his sword, on the ridge along the blade, one other unidentifiable place and that the name of the god Tyr should be carved twice.[55] She also teaches him that he needs to learn 'sea runes' to avoid shipwreck, 'healing runes', 'speech runes', 'thought runes', 'ale runes' to seduce another man's wife and 'saving runes' to assist difficult childbirth.[56]

The writer and Heathen activist Freya Aswynn[57] (a living embodiment of the Valkyrie current if ever I saw one!) points out that in the story Sigdrifa / Brunnhilde becomes a power in her own right, independent of Odin and creating her own wyrd. All that Odin can do is put the situation on hold until Sigurd is available, and at that point she becomes the teacher of magic to him (just as Freyja did for Odin.)

Völundarkviða
This has the Swan Maiden story told in Chapter 1, and names Hlaðguðr Svanhvít and Hervör Alvitr as well as Ölrún.

Völuspá
A völva (a type of seeress / magician) informs Odin of her seeing Valkyries: Skuld, Skögul, Gunnr, Hild, Gondul and Geirskögul who she terms as 'Ladies of the War Lord who are ready to ride as Valkyries over all the Earth. (Stanza 31)

On all sides saw I Valkyries assemble,
Ready to ride to the ranks of the gods;
Skuld bore the shield, and Skogul rode next,
Guth, Hild, Gondul, and Geirskogul.
Of Herjan's maidens the list have ye heard,
Valkyries ready to ride o'er the earth.

Younger (Prose) Edda

This was written by Snorri Sturlusson in 13th century Iceland, but draws upon some older (sometimes lost) earlier sources.[58] There are references to Valkyries in the following sections: Eiríksmál, Gylfaginning, Skáldskaparmál and Húsdrápa. Snorri quotes many poems from the Elder (Poetic) Edda, but mainly only as fragmentary excerpts. Some translations offer fuller versions from it.

Eiríksmál

This 10th century poem (also quoted in Fagrskinna) has the lines said by Odin translated into English as:

What sort of dream is that, Odin?
I dreamed I rose up before dawn
to clear up Val-hall for slain people.
I aroused the Einherjar,
bade them get up to strew the benches,
clean the beer-cups,
the valkyries to serve wine
for the arrival of a prince

From this it appears that the dead warriors (Einherjar) have to clear up their own mess in the morning before going off to fight again, leaving the Valkyries to serve wine. Wine is a high status drink, more expensive than mead or beer at that period. This story is also told in Heimskringla where it is explained that Eirik Bloodaxe and five other kings arrive. The noise they make arriving is mistaken by the god Bragi as Balder or a whole army.

Gylfaginning

King Gylfi (in his disguised form of Gangleri) is told about Valkyries by Odin in his disguised character 'High.' He is told that they have a duty to serve in Valhalla, in charge of serving food and drink. He lists the names of several Valkyries in an excerpt from Grímnismál. He adds that they are sent by Odin (himself in reality) to every battle to choose who is to die and who have victory, especially mentioning Róta, Gunnr and Skuld in that capacity. It is interesting to note that he says that is they who decide the outcome of the battle, whilst one may expect from other sources for him to say that was the decision of Odin himself. Later he mentions that the Valkyries attend Balder's funeral with Odin, Frigg and the ravens.

Skáldskaparmál & Húsdrápa

The poem relates how Sigmund's son Helgi Hundingsbane agreed to take Sigrún the Valkyrie daughter of Högni as his wife against her unwilling betrothal to Hodbrodd son of Granmar the king of Södermanland. A fuller version occurs in the paragraphs below.

Within Skáldskaparmál there is a quotation from a poem Húsdrápa by the skald (poet) Úlfr Uggason who lived in the 10th century. Describing Balder's funeral feast he says:

> *There I perceive valkyries and ravens,*
> *accompanying the wise victory-tree*
> *to the drink of the holy offering.*

'Victory tree' is believed to indicate Odin, and these lines seem to reinforce the information given in Gylfaginning (above.)

Hrafnsmál[59]

This is thought to be composed by Þorbjörn Hornklofi, a Norwegian skald of the 9th century. In the course of telling about the life and deeds of Harald 1st (Fairhair) of Norway a Valkyrie talks to a raven. She is described as having white arms (a sign of refinement through not working in the fields) golden hair, sparkling eyes and high- minded and not interested in male company. She is wise enough to be able to speak with the bird, whose name forms part of the works title 'Hrafn.'

By now you should have noticed numerous references to ravens being involved in stories with Valkyries. I pose the question: is it just they both select from the battlefield, or does a Valkyrie have some extra special affinity or link with them? The qualities of the raven and other related corvids such as the crow have been investigated in recent years, and they have been found to be the most intelligent of the bird species; not just using tools[60] but designing plans before they solve and tackle a problem.[61] Corvids are also known to bring their mates small gifts, and in one exceptional recent case a young lady in Seattle that regularly fed crows in her garden was brought gifts by them.[62] Ravens have similar problem solving and tool using behaviour and communicate large food sources to each other.[63] They also have an affinity with wolves: they need them to break into large carcases but in return give an alarm to the wolf if danger threatens.[64]

They also seem to hold some form of memory for those who help or hinder them, as in an experiment at Seattle College Campus USA[65]. There is the Old English term 'crâwe' for crow and 'hræfn' and 'hremn' for raven, so it seems that they did distinguish between the two. Modern English gives us at least three collective nouns for a flock of crows: murder, conspiracy and unkindness, which all have negative connotations.

A Valkyrie speaks with a raven by Anthony Frederick Sandys (1862)

Of course the ravens Huginn and Muninn are Odin's scouts around the world, whose names translate as 'thought' and 'memory'. He says that he fears for 'Thought' but for 'Memory' even greater in the Grímnismál - Lay of Grímnir. If you think about it you do not exist as an individual without memories, which would disable you from having many future thoughts anyway without some structure provided from your personal history.

Vikings have sometimes been described as fighting under a raven banner. In **Orkneyingsaga** the mother of Earl Sigurd Hlodvirsson weaves a magical raven banner that will enable him to defeat odds of 7:1 in war, but it has the cost that the standard bearer will die.[66]

The poem is in the Elder (Poetic) Edda but much quoted by Sturlusson in the Prose (Younger) Edda. Sturlusson calls Odin Hrafnaguð (raven god) in Gylfaginning 37, and elsewhere in the skaldic poem Haustlǫng Odin receives the title Hrafnáss (raven- As i.e. the raven god.)

Heimskringla

This book[67] is also by Snorri Sturlusson who wrote the Younger Prose Edda, and is mainly a history of the Earls of Orkney, but contains a lot of magical and mythological material. It contains Hákonarmál by the 10th century skald Eyvindr skáldaspillir, in praise of King Hakon I of Norway who died after a battle. Although nominally a Christian he instructs that as he has died among Heathens that they bury him in whatever way seems right to them. They take his body to Sæheim in North Hordaland and bury him in full armour under a large mound with Heathen prayers 'to speed him to Valhalla.' As Ellis-Davidson[68] states:

> In a funeral poem celebrating the death of King Hakon of Norway in the tenth century, the valkyries are described as dignified figures on horseback, wise in demeanour. (Hákonarmál 11)

Odin sends Göndul and Skögul, two of his Valkyries to choose among the Kings followers and Göndul is seen leaning upon her spear, sitting on horseback with helmet and shield. She tells Hakon that the result of the battle was fated against him but she will ride to Valhalla to tell Odin that the King will be joining him as one of his einherjar to face the awful Fenris wolf at Ragnarok.

This story presents some questions: why would a Christian king be selected for Valhalla? Did the fact that he chose to let his comrades bury him in a Heathen fashion constitute him symbolically turning his back on Christianity and returning to Heathenism?

Valkyries Skögul and Geirskögul seem to duplicate each other's actions in Heimskringla but appear as separate names in several other texts. Göndul and Skögul are sent by Odin to select warriors for Valhalla.

Other Old Norse Poetry

There is some poetry not incorporated into the Poetic Edda:

The Lay of Harold[69] is a heroic poem about King Harold of Norway (c.860-933 CE) constructed from fragments found in Fagrskinna.[70] Unusually it consists of a conversation between a Valkyrie and a raven, and shows that she can understand its' speech as she asks it questions.

Hákonarmál

The Lay of Hákon is also in Fagrskinna as well as being contained in Heimskringla. It features Skogul the Valkyrie escorting the king to Valhalla and answering questions about him. As Hollander[71] intimates, the poet Eyvindr (skáldaspillir) Finnsson is probably trying to rehabilitate the Heathen reputation of his Norwegian king with his subjects, as he had at one stage embraced Christianity. King Hákon the Good of Norway died in 961 CE so this must have been composed soon after.

> *Hear the lofty lords of war,*
> *How the Valkyries speak,*
> *Maidens, mounted on horseback,*
> *Winsome horse lords,*
> *Wearing high helms,*
> *And holding shields as shelter.*

Medieval German text

Nibelungenlied

Mention 'The Nibelungenlied'[72] to the average person and they look at you blankly. Yet mention 'The Ring Cycle' and they may well identify it as a lengthy suite of operas by Wagner. That in many ways is unfortunate, because the former (in Middle High German) gives the unaltered source of the story, without Wagner's subsequent additions, renaming of characters etc.

It is believed to have been written between 1190 -1205 by an anonymous poet, probably in the area of the Danube near Vienna, and survives in differing versions in a number of manuscripts. Some of the story is very similar to Old Norse stories contained in the Elder and Younger Edda's, Völsunga saga, the Legend of Norna-Gest, and the Þiðrekssaga. Several of the characters are drawn from real life historical figures and events such as the defeat of the Burgundians in 436 CE and a dispute in 6th century Merovingia. Central to the story is the Queen / Valkyrie Brünhild and Sigurd, as told in Chapter 3.

Old English texts

The word wælcyrge occurs most often in the manuscript MS cotton Cleopatra III, where it is used as a 'gloss' to translate Latin texts. The manuscript is believed to date from about 930 CE.[73] Much later the word occurs in the Danish ruler of England Cnut's Proclamation of 1020, part of which translates as

> *For it is as the bishops say, that it is very much with God to be amended if one breaks an oath or a pledge. Further, they declare that we ought, with all our might and all our main, seek and love and honour God, who*

is mild, and all of us must avoid unrighteousness, the deeds of kinslayers, manslayers and murderers and perjurers and witches and Valkyries and adulterers and incests.

This warning to avoid the wrath of the Christian God by not sinning appears to class Valkyries with other human sinners. A similar association is made in the sermon Sermo Lupi ad Anglos[74], (Sermon of the Wolf) written by the Archbishop of Canterbury Wulfstan II in about 1014, the word wælcyrian is used, and considered to appear as plural word for a human "sorceress." The line reads:

her syndan wiccan & wælcyrian
here there are witches and sorceresses

'Sermon of the Wolf' was written when England was under Viking attacks which he interprets as a punishment from the Christian God. Ewing[75] makes the point that Valkyries are in the context of the sermon being categorised as real women here, not supernatural entities.

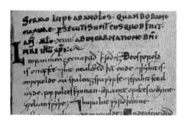

A part of the Sermon of the Wolf manuscript.

From about the same period a text by another cleric Aldhelm equates wælcyrge with ueneris, a term for the classic Furies of earlier mythology.[76]

Elsewhere the Roman Goddess Bellona is labelled 'wælcyrge' and a raven flying over the Egyptian army is described as 'wonn wælceaseg' which has been translated as 'dark one choosing the slain.'[77]

An Old English translation of The Wonders of the East (contained in Cotton Tiberius BV manuscript) uses the word with a connotation of monstrous; a fantastic creature is described with 'wælkyrian eagan' – the eyes of a Valkyrie. Elsewhere it describes a place with Gorgons present as wælcyrginc i.e. Valkyrie like. Clearly the Anglo Saxon Valkyries seem to have developed petrifying gazes independently from their Scandinavian counterparts.

The fact that the words wælcyrie and wælcyrge occur in Old English texts suggests that Anglo Saxons may have had a belief in them, albeit slightly different or even confused to that of Old Norse texts; they certainly seem to use the words in a different context in places. Whether that was due to the ignorance of Christian writers being confused or ignorant about Heathen beliefs, or whether a different understanding was current it is impossible to say with any certainty. Experts are unable to agree whether the terms were part of the original Germanic culture imported into England with the arrival of Saxons, Jutes and Angles in the 6th century or whether they were copied from Vikings in the early 9th century.

The Christian monk and historian Bede included a lot of information about Pagan customs within his writings, including the origins for calendar months and days. Kathleen Herbert[78] comments that 'Hreð was a wælcyrie; her month was the last month of winter.' (March) However, earlier in the same paragraph she quotes Bede as stating that Hreð's month was 'named after their goddess Rheda, to whom they sacrificed in that month.' As she also says, Hreð means fierce, cruel or rough which can describe the weather at that time of year as much as the character of a wælcyrie. I am not convinced that

a Valkyrie was the same as a major goddess to be
worshipped.

Carving from Urnes stave church, Norway

Chapter 6 Information from the Icelandic sagas.

I have separated the sagas from the rest of the literary sources, (although they frequently overlap and reference each other) as they are sometimes a very different type of resource deriving from stories of the settlers of Iceland and Greenland. In splitting material I have tried to avoid duplication between chapters, but do be aware that there is sometimes more than one source of information. Many do contain verifiable facts such as locations and names, but have some elements that we are less likely to be able to verify. Some were once thought to be nearly fairy stories by academics until modern evidence proved that they have some basis of fact. E.g. The Saga of Eirik the Red contains the story of his son Leif Eriksson sailing to a country Vinland identified as part of North America, long before the Pilgrim Fathers or Saint Brendan in about 1000 CE. Some of academia had to revise its position of disbelief when physical evidence of Viking artefacts were found in L'Anse aux Meadows, Newfoundland in 1960.

Grottasongr

This story of a miraculous mill that will not stop grinding appears in some manuscripts of Snorri's Edda, but is not included within all of them. In stanza 13 two females forced to work it says:

> *And since we two*
> *in Sweden*
> *far-sighted, both of us,*
> *Strode into battle.*
> *We baited bears*
> *And hacked at shields,*
> *Marched right through*
> *Their mail-clad host.*

One could be forgiven for identifying these characters as Valkyries, but within context they appear to be giantesses, albeit taking on Valkyrie like behaviour. Tolley[79] forms this opinion and I have no reason to disagree with it. I do wonder if the 'bears' they bated were berserkers, the elite warrior caste that adopted a bear totem and frenzied fighting technique.

Groenlendinga saga

Freydís, a central character in both Groenlendinga saga[80] and Eiríks saga rauða wears men's clothes and uses an axe to brutally murder five other women. That doesn't make her a Valkyrie but shows that it was believed that there were some violent women about during the saga age.

Saga of King Hrolf Kraki

This saga[81] contains a higher proportion of magical and mythological content than most as well as frequent killings, inadvertent incest and battles. In it the Queen of Saxland (Saxony) wears a coat of mail and carries a sword and shield. She is a feisty character, full of tricks and magic with a streak of cruelty but there is no direct evidence for her actually being a Valkyrie.

Njáls saga[82]

In chapter 157 a man called Dörruð sees twelve valkyries go into a hut at Caithness, Scotland and spies upon them. A section of the poem is given in Chapter 1 of this book, describing how Norns weave with skulls as weights, entrails as thread, a sword as the shuttle and then pull apart their work to decide the fate of warriors at Battle of Clontarf. The threads' reels were made of arrows. They depart riding their horses bareback, brandishing swords and singing war chants.

> *Now awful it is to be without,*
> *as blood-red rack races overhead;*
> *is the welkin gory with warriors' blood*
> *as we valkyries war-songs chanted*

(stanza 9)

In the poem "The Song of the Valkyries" apart from the horrific weaving scene we have the Valkyries chanting charms around the King's son to protect him.

Saga of Thidrandi.

This tale forms part of the **Saga of Olaf Tryggvason** in **Flateyjarbók.**[83]

Thidrandi is portrayed as a modest and well liked young man. His father Hall had troubling prophetic dreams, and forbade anyone to leave the hall where they were feasting with his friend Thorhall Seer once the door was barred for the night. However, Thidrandi heard a knocking at the door during the night and thought it was late arrivals. He went out, sword in hand and saw nine women in dark clothes with drawn swords arriving from the north. Nine more in bright clothes came from the south. Although he defended himself he was attacked severely. In the morning his father found him mortally wounded. Thidrandi told him what had happened to him before he died.

Thorhall Seer interpreted this as a new faith coming to Iceland; the dark riders were ancestral spirits connected to the old Heathen ways taking a sacrifice before they made way for a new religion. The light riders had tried to defend him but had arrived too late.

It is not specified that the riders are Valkyries, but they ride in the magical number of nine and bear swords. It would be an isolated case for Valkyries to actually fight with swords compared with other stories we have about them.[84]

Other Sagas

There are several other sagas that mention Valkyries or allude to them without directly telling us more about them, including information about Disir. Included in those are:

Egils Saga[85] refers to 'Valkyrie armour' in verse 24 and later mentions a dísablót (ritual to honour the Disir) being held in Atloy when King Eirik and his Queen Gunnhild arrive.

Grettir's Saga[86] refers to 'Valkyrie arts' meaning war in verse 27.

King Heidrik's Saga [87]tells of the king defeating his father in law Harald in battle and offering the dead to Odin. His wife Helga reacts to her father's death by hanging herself 'in the Hall of the Dis.'

Saga of the People of Laxardal[88] refers to Gudrun who is descended from a Valkyrie.

Saga of Gunnlaug Serpent Tongue[89] refers to a 'spear sister' (Valkyrie) and 'tree of the Valkyrie' which could mean Odin, a warrior, horse or something else.

Gisli Sursson's Saga[90] has at least three Valkyrie references:
"I saw the Valkyrie hand reed (sword) covered in blood" in verse 6.
"I had to defend myself against Valkyries derision" in verse 8.
"Valkyries dire battle plan" in verse 9.

Ynglinga Saga[91] contains information about the death of King Athils. It says that as he was attending the sacrifice to the Disir at Uppsala (Sweden.) he was thrown from his horse as he rode it about in the hall of the Goddess. This confirms reports from elsewhere that there was a temple dedicated to the Disir there, and that rites were held to honour them. From other sources it is believed that the dísablót (the Disirs' sacrifice) was either held at Winterfinding in October (as mentioned in **Viga-Glums Saga**[92] or near to Yule in December. There is a Germanic / Anglo Saxon festival known as modraniht ('Mother's Night'), which took place around the end of December and that may either be the direct equivalent of dísablót or purely a continuation of the extensive North European three matrons cult. However, Disting in Sweden seems to be a similar festival and that doesn't fall until February. If one believes that some Valkyries were drawn from the ranks of the Disir, this could be significant.

Incidentally was the act of riding his horse into the temple seen as profaning it? It doesn't say.[93] Certainly when in 627 CE the Heathen priest Coifi bore weapons, rode a stallion instead of a mare to a temple and threw a spear in it before setting it alight at Goodmanham it was seen as a very public display of going against previous taboos and setting an example to the subjects of King Edwin of Northumbria to embrace Christianity.[94] Carrying weapons into temples of many religions has also generally been against their rules, including in Heathen Iceland, although there the goði (priest) was allowed to keep and ride a stallion as we find in **Hrafnkel's saga**[95]. A priest of the god Frey called Hrafnkell Freysgoði kills a man who rides his sacred stallion Freyfaxi without permission.

Disir appear to be attached to some family clans as a sort of protective spirit, and in several tales people dream of them communicating someone's fate, such as in the **Poem of Atli**[96] from Greenland. A lady named Glaumvor predicts her husband Atli's death by recounting a dream of women coming to her dressed in mourning clothes and summoning Atli to their mead benches – another pointer to the behaviour of Valkyries choosing heroes for their halls. This scene is repeated in the **Saga of the Volsungs.**[97]

Hlaf's Saga[98] tells of a warrior called Utsteinn taunting his enemy that 'his Disir 'will ensure victory, but is met with a rebuttal that suggests that they have already been beaten by Hlaf's own Disir. This tends to show Disir in a more warlike mode than usual, (acting like Valkyries) and having particular sympathies for one force or another.

Jómsvikinga Saga[99]

Earl Hákon is outnumbered and offers prayers to his 'protector' Ðorgerðr Hölgabrúðr which are rejected. He finally sacrificed his own seven year old son Erlingr to appease her.

The opposing fleet of Jómsviking ships were interfered with by an ethereal figure called Ðorgerðr Hölgabrúðr who sent violent hail storms to rain down upon them.

> *Hárvard the Hewer was first to see*
> *Ðorgerðr Hölgabrúðr above the fleet of Earl Hákon,*
> *and then many second sighted men saw her,*
> *though other men could not see*

The leader Sigvaldi said that not everyone can see her, just those with 'second sight.' It is unclear from the story whether the attacker is a Valkyrie or some other force such as a witch, hamingja (a transferable luck or success that can project into a physical form) or fylga, a type of supernatural 'fetch' that is magically sent ahead of the person intentionally. Both of these are part of Heathen beliefs within certain cultures and time periods. N.B. The two terms are contested and frequently confused with each other.

Valkyrie greeting mounted warrior from Tissø, Denmark

Statue of Valkyrie by Stephen Sinding (1908) in the Churchill Park,
Kastellet Copenhagen Denmark.

Chapter 7 Charms, Curses and Riddles

Some charms contain elements of their Heathen origins despite being later Christianised. In a time of one faith replacing or overlaying another it may have been more pragmatic of the Christian church to do this rather than unrealistically forbid people to use them, especially if there was no direct Christian substitute or equivalent. The fact that some people such as the East Angles King Raedwald saw no problem with setting up a Christian altar alongside his Heathen ones[100] demonstrates that attitudes were not as fixed or prescriptive at the time of the initial conversion of the English kingdoms around 620-650 CE. Kings and bishops were still issuing laws against Heathen practices 400 years later can be seen as evidence that those beliefs and practices were still happening amongst the common folk (albeit in secret) for long after the countries official conversion to Christianity. One does not usually create new laws against things that no longer happen.

Wið Færstice
This is a charm in Old English to cure a sudden pain or stitch:

> They were loud, yes, loud,
> when they rode over the (burial) mound;
> they were fierce when they rode across the land.
> Shield yourself now, you can survive this strife.
> Out, little spear, if there is one here within.
> It stood under/behind lime-wood (i.e. a shield), under a
> light-coloured/light-weight shield,
> where those mighty women marshalled their powers,
> and they send shrieking spears

The last line appears to refer to Valkyries, although does not use the actual word, referring to them as 'mighty women' instead. Richard North[101] suggests that this interpretation is likely whilst H.E. Davidson[102] goes further in suggesting that the lines may have originated in a battle spell, since reduced to a lesser function.

In a similar way the term 'victory women' (sigewif) has also been interpreted as the presence of Valkyries in an Old English charm to settle a swarm of bees, or even the bees with their stings being seen as like Valkyries and their spears:

> *Settle down, victory-women,*
> *never be wild and fly to the woods.*
> *Be as mindful of my welfare,*
> *as is each man of eating and of home.*

Merseberg Charms

The 1st Merseberg Charm refers to Idisi fixing and releasing fetters on an army:

> *Once the Idisi sat, sat here and there,*
> *some bound fetters, some hampered the army,*
> *some untied fetters:*
> *Escape from the fetters, flee from the enemies.*

Rudolf Simek[103] indicates that he considers the Old Norse term Idisi (Old English Idis) to be a form of Valkyrie, and cites the Herfjötur Valkyrie name as being Old Norse for 'army fetter.'

Ragnhild Tregagás charm

There was a trial of a woman called Ragnhild Tregagás in Bergen, Norway in 1324.[104] She was accused of witchcraft, with an accusation that she had tried to end the marriage of her former partner Bard to his new wife. It was alleged that she had recited a verse calling upon Göndul (a Valkyrie) and two un-named others to do harm:

I send out from me the spirits of Gondul.
May the first bite you in the back.
May the second bite you in the breast.
May the third turn hate and envy upon you.

Choosing to use the Valkyrie name Gondul out of all the ones available seems appropriate. She is the only one of the few with a name that directly suggests magic in its translated form of 'enchanted stave.'

A Valkyries Curse from Helgakviða Hundingsbana II
Although Ragnhild Tregagás charm (above) has been termed a charm, it is more properly a curse i.e. a spell of ill intent. The following is a full on, no - holds barred vindictive curse made by the Valkyrie Sigrún upon her brother Dagr. He has killed her husband Helgi after having his life spared by him and swearing allegiance to him. He sacrificed to Odin who gave him a special spear to do it at a place called Fjöturlund. This shows Odin working against the interests of one of his Valkyries, and there are other times he is shown to be disloyal or unreliable to friends.

Now may every
oath thee bite
That with Helgi
sworn thou hast,
By the water
bright of Leipt,
And the ice-cold
stone of Uth.

The ship shall sail not
in which thou sailest,
Though a favouring wind

shall follow after;
The horse shall run not
whereon thou ridest,
Though fain thou art
thy foe to flee.

The sword shall bite not
which thou bearest,
Till thy head itself
it sings about.
Vengeance were mine
for Helgi's murder,
Wert thou a wolf
in the woods without,
Possessing nought
and knowing no joy,
Having no food
save corpses to feed on

A Runic Stave charm

There is a 14th century four sided 'Valkyrie stick' charm amongst the Bryggen inscriptions found in Bergen, Norway. It has runic inscriptions indicating:

I carve cure-runes
Help-runes, once against elves, twice against trolls,
thrice against thurs.

It is then a Valkyrie is mentioned:

Against the harmful skag-valkyrie,
so that she never shall, though she never would -
evil woman! - injure your life.

*I send you, I look at you, wolfish perversion, and
unbearable desire,
may distress descend on you and jötuns wrath.
Never shall you sit, never shall you sleep ... until you
love me as yourself.*

The beginning of the charm is similar to the opening of
Sigrdrífumál. In that the Valkyrie Sigrdrífa teaches rune lore. In
the first verse it seems to give protection to the intended
recipient. However in the second stanza it appears to aim at
torturing the intended victim until they fall back in love with the
sender. (There does not seem to be an agreed meaning for
the term 'skag' in skag-valkyrie.) Interestingly the verses
predate the later Sigrdrífumál by a century, possibly showing
that the oral tradition was keeping it alive.[105]

Riddles
There is one other speculative source of Anglo Saxon
knowledge of a wælcyrie: Phillip Purser[106] believes that the
answers to two of the riddles contained in the Exeter Book[107]
are a wælcyrie:

Riddle 72
*Ic wæs fæmne geong feax har cwene,
Ond ænlic rinc on ane tid;
Fleah mid fulgum and on flode swom,
Deaf under yþe dead mid fiscum,
Ond on foldon stop hæfde ferð cwicu.*

*I was a young woman, a grey-haired queen,
At the same time, a peerless warrior;
Flew with birds, swam in the sea,
Dove under wave, dead among fishes,
And on land stepped, possessed of a living soul*

The suggestion here is that a warrior woman who can fly and swim must be a Valkyrie.

Riddle 8

Wiga is on eorþan wundrum acenned
dryhtum to nytte of dumbum twam
torht atyhted þone on teon wigeð
feond his feonde fer strangne oft
wif hine wrið

.

A warrior is wondrously brought into the world
for the use of lords by two dumb things;
brightly extracted, which for his hurt
foe bears against foe. Strong though he is
a woman binds him.

The suggestion is that the 'woman who binds him' is a Valkyrie putting on war fetters.

Flat Valkyrie figure from Sweden

Chapter 8. Monuments, pendants and other artefacts

Female figures.

Silver pendants that may have been considered protective amulets have been found in Viking female graves. Some bear drinking horns and have been interpreted as Valkyrie figures or alternatively Disir female ancestor representations.

 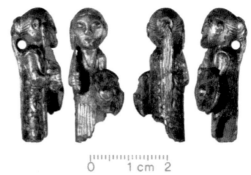

Figure from Birka, Sweden   Figure from Hårby on Funen, Denmark

A three dimensional figure dated to around 800 CE from Hårby, Denmark has long hair tied in a knot and is carrying a sword and shield. She has a floor length gown. It is now in Odense Museum.[108]

There is also a copper alloy pendant from Cawthorpe, near Bourne in Lincolnshire England, with a female holding a spear and a shield as well as having a sheathed sword hanging at her side.

A group of brooches from the 9-10th century known as 'Valkyrie and horseman' type are spread widely across the areas that Vikings settled. A cast bronze example with openwork was found in Nottingham. The horseman faces right with a spear in his right hand. A robed female figure faces him with a shield on her left arm.[109]

Monumental stones

U1163

Uppland figure offering horn

Tjängvide image stone

Rök stone

Tängelgårda stone

Hunninge stone

There are Valkyries referred to on a couple of monumental rune stones: **Karlevi Runestone** on the island of Öland, Sweden, mentions the Valkyrie Þrúðr. It is believed to date from the 10th century. On another stone known as the **Rök Runestone** from Östergötland, Sweden there is a kenning (synonym) in the text for a Valkyrie riding a wolf. That stone is dated to the 9th century and has coded runic messages on all four sides and the top. The interpretation of it has been complex and controversial. For a good summary of the arguments see Harris.[110]

A rune stone catalogued as **U1163** originated in Drävle but was moved to its present location in Göksbo, Sweden long ago. The picture on it features Sigurd putting his sword through a dragon. Also present are the dwarf Andvari and the

Valkyrie Sigrdrífa offering him drink. The stone was erected by the family of a man called Erinbjôrn.

The well- known image of Odin on his eight legged horse Sleipnir being offered a drinking horn by a Valkyrie is from the **Tjängvide image stone** from the island of Gotland, just off Sweden. She is wearing a long dress with an apron and carrying a shield in her left hand and a drawn sword in her right hand.

The **Hunninge Image Stone** from Gotland is currently on display at the Fornsalen Museum in Visby. It shows a woman greeting a horse rider warrior, and it has been thought that it could represent Sigurd and Brunhilde. There is another similar woman by a representation of Gunnar in the snake pit. The stone is well known for its detailed central picture of a sailing ship as is the **Broa image stone** that is surmounted by a female figure offering a horn to a mounted warrior. The stone is from Broa in Halla on the island of Gotland dated to 700-800 CE.[111]

Interestingly there is also a memorial stone for a woman called Ailikn from Uddvide who is shown in a horse drawn waggon being greeted by a Valkyrie with mead horn, which suggests that women received similar treatment from them after death.[112]

Jesch[113] identifies the story on the **Tängelgårda stone** from Lärbro parish, Gotland, Sweden as that of a funeral procession of horseback warriors holding rings, and the hero entering Valhalla. She comments that when Họgni, the father of the abducted Hildr tries to rescue her

> *'she went between the two sides with false messages and egged them onto fight, discouraging attempts at a settlement. The battle continued all day and at night*

Hildr woke up all the slain to life so that the battle could continue the next day, and the next day.'

The battle is doomed to continue until the end of time, and of course the woman is a Valkyrie with a name that translates as 'battle.' Given her story it is a wonder that she wasn't called 'Trouble!'

Franks Casket.
This ornately carved 7th century whale bone box (probably made in Northumbria) is held in the British Museum. The decorations on each of the five panels (sides and lid) illustrate different stories. A female is pictured as seated behind a warrior on the lid, and another with a bird's head is offering drink beside a burial mound on a side panel have been identified as Valkyries by Prof. K Hauck and Hilda Ellis Davidson.[114]

The inscription on the side panel has been translated as "Here Hos sits on the sorrow mound; she suffers distress in that Ertae had decreed for her a wretched den of sorrows and torments of the mind."[115] But who are Hos and her tormenter Ertae? Hos does not feature in the lists of Valkyrie names, and signifies ideas such as escort or company. In that sense she could be the escort (wife) of the person in the mound, killed by Ertae, whoever (or whatever) he is. If the inscription is connected with the illustration (which would seem reasonable given that there is a mound in it) the identity of Hos being a Valkyrie would seem doubtful; Valkyries are not usually known for being sorrowful around burial mounds. There is of course the comparable Old Norse magical practice of utiseta (sitting out) on a mound for communication with the supernatural, but I am unaware of any recorded similar Anglo Saxon practice.

It is believed that the lid panel shows Egil (ON Agilaz) the brother of Völundr fending off foes with his archery. (Völundr / Wayland Smith is shown on the front panel) The female is seated in a house behind him, and appears to be holding either a sword or distaff by the middle. From the tale of Egil one might presume her to be his wife Aliruna or Ölrún the Wise, a daughter of Kiár of Valland. Her name does appear as a Valkyrie within Völundarkviða, part of the Poetic Edda contained within the Codex Regius. Presumably the reason for Ölrún to have a birds head is to show her in her original form as a swan maiden.

I am conscious that there are several contradictory interpretations of the casket, especially the runic inscriptions. I do not intend to add to them with further ones of my own, although some of them are interesting and enlightening.[116]

Hadrian's Wall, England.
At a point on the wall known to the Romans as Vercovicium, there are three votive stones forming part of a shrine to their war god Mars. However, the inscriptions made by some Frisian soldiers serving in the army (Germanic tribesmen, Tuihantian citizens of the Cuneus of Frisians) are also dedicated to the two Alaisiagae which they name as Bede and Fimmilenae. On another inscription they refer to the two Alaisiagae as Boudihillia and Friagabis.

These inscriptions have caused much speculation amongst scholars, some of whom believe them to refer to prototypes from which the later Norse Valkyries developed from. I do not intend to get drawn into that debate, but there is a good analysis of the merits of different experts' opinions made by Purser.[117] A carving on one of the stones show a robed woman with one hand held in a triumphal gesture whilst the other partly conceals a sword in the folds of her dress.

Oseberg Tapestry
Judith Jesch suggests that some female figures on this tapestry may be interpreted as Valkyries. The tapestry was part of a high status female burial from no later than 834 CE at Vestfold, Norway. The burial contained an elaborately carved waggon and fine ship, sledges, horses and many other artefacts including other rare textile finds.[118] They are preserved in the Viking Ship Museum in Oslo.

Reconstructed Oseberg tapestry

Chapter 9 Inspiration

Whilst hopefully I and others have established that Valkyries were an important element of beliefs within the Norse and Anglo Saxon worlds, it has to be admitted that values, religions and cultures have changed since that period from over 1000 years ago. So do we still need Valkyries? From popular modern culture the answer would seem to be 'yes.' Marketing men do not invest their advertising budgets in associating their products with concepts that do not strike a chord with their prospective customers.

Valkyries are powerful symbols that have inspired many people to use the associated ideas of awesome, sinister, powerful women with everything from a Honda Goldwing Valkyrie motorbike to art and poetry, beer and music. To list all the poetry and artwork that feature the imagery of Valkyries would be a fairly lengthy but meaningless task, and of course they mean different things to a variety of people. The dark forbidding imagery is balanced by the more beautiful ethereal forms of some romantic Victorian artists, and the art that Arthur Rackham created is a major influence on my personal vision of them despite also personally acknowledging their more visceral bloodthirsty nature.

Their images have also been featured in manga art, trading cards and graphic novels and comics. Their powerful force has not been neglected by the creators of fantasy role player games such as World of Warcraft or rock musicians such as the American heavy rock band Valkyrie. A young adult novel by Ingrid Paulson 'Valkyrie Rising'[119] has been very successful and has inspired other writers to explore a similar theme.

'Valkyrie' is a 2008 film and book inspired by the Operation Valkyrie 20th July plot against Hitler by some of his officers during World War II. The plan was to assassinate him and take control of Germany via a National Emergency Plan, but it failed. The book 'The Valkyrie Operation' by Wensley Clarkson[120] is about a completely different sort of secret mission: the apparently true life story of Jonathan Moyle, an agent murdered whilst spying for the British on Chilean attempts at illegal arms dealing to Iraq. Coincidentally there is a 127mm multiple rocket launcher aptly called the Valkyrie.

1901 Jugendstil beer advertisement

Just as there are archetypal figures in stories based upon the twelve Jungian character types that change, merge, regenerate etc. a system of twelve corresponding archetypes has been proposed to categorise branding of products: Sage, Innocent, Explorer, Ruler, Creator, Caregiver, Magician, Hero, Outlaw, Lover, Jester, and Regular Guy/Girl.[121] I think that you can work out where most of the products pitch within those archetypes, but I find it interesting that Valkyries as a branding could include several of them. However an archetype derived from a different source may be more relevant: I am thinking of the 'Wild Woman' archetype proposed by Clarissa Pinkola Estés[122] which includes many guises.

NASA has an advanced military robot called Valkyrie[123] and that is also the name of what is claimed to be the fastest piston engine aircraft on the market built by Cobalt[124] as well as a Saunders Roe Valkyrie wooden seaplane of 1926.

The image of a strong female has been frequently connected with: there is a female body builders' website,[125] a women's wrestling company and any number of other company names using the concept. I was interested to read a very personal dual language book by Icelandic playwright, motorcyclist, Heathen and author Guðrún Kristin called Óðsmál[126] which bring together her feelings as a strong independent woman in identifying with her countries past and its mythology.

I started this book with a mention of 'Ride of the Valkyries' as the one thing that most of the public can most readily mention in connection with Valkyries. It seems somehow appropriate to comment upon it here at the end.

'The Ride of the Valkyries' (German: *Walkürenritt* or *Ritt der Walküren)* comes from the opening of Act 3 of the opera Die Walküre, which is the second of a suite of four operas by Wagner collectively known as Der Ring des Nibelungen or the Ring Cycle. Originally Richard Wagner tried to stop 'Ride of the Valkyries' being performed seperately, wanting to keep it within context but from the time the whole work was played in Munich,1870 until its enthusiastic reception at Bayreuth in 1876 he was bombarded with requests for it to be used. He eventually gave in and even performed it as an encore himself.[127]

Since then the tune has become the very appropriate regimental quick march for the British Parachute Regiment and was used to chilling effect for the helicopter sequences in the successful film 'Apocalypse Now' of 1979.

Regardless of the many competing ideas that have been associated with them, Valkyries continue to portray a strong independent female image and remain a fascinating feature of Heathen mythology and beliefs. I believe that becoming more familiar with their ways and identity is a valuable component to the growth of a man or woman's spiritual path, particularly within modern Heathenism. How one relates to them is an individual choice, but long may they continue to be well respected figures of awe.

Pete Jennings 2016

Ride of the Valkyries by Henry de Groux, c.1890

Select Bibliography

Anon. (1991) *Beowulf* (trans. J Porter) Little Downham: Anglo Saxon Books

Anon. (1996) *The Poetic Edda.* (trans C. Larrington,) Oxford: Oxford University Press

Anon. (2015) Valkyrie. *Encyclopædia Britannica Online.* Retrieved 02 November, 2015, from http://www.britannica.com/topic/Valkyrie-Norse-mythology

Aswynn, F. (1990) *Leaves of Yggdrasil.* USA: Llewellyn

Ballard, S. (2007) 15. Stirring Women, Weapons and Weaving: Aspects of gender identity and symbols of power in early Anglo Saxon England.in Hamilton, Whitehouse & Wright (Eds.) *The Archaeology of Women.* Walnut Creek CA: Left Coast Press

Bauschatz, P. (1982) *The Well and the Tree: World and Time in Early Germanic Culture* USA: University of Massachusetts Press

Bayerschmidt & Hollander (1998) *Njal's Saga.* Ware: Wordsworth Classics

Becker, A. (2006) Fylgia and Valkyrie: the warriors companions in life and death. *Wiðowinde* journal 1(141) 22-26

Bede (1951) *The Ecclesiastical History of the English Nation.* (Trans. J Stevens) London: JM Dent & Sons Ltd

Bellows, H. (1936) *The Poetic Edda.* www.sacred-texts.com

Branston, B. (1974) *The Lost Gods of England.* London: Thames & Hudson

Byock, J. (1998) *The Saga of King Hrolf Kraki* London: Penguin

Byock, J. (1990) *The Saga of the Volsungs.* USA: University of California

Chantepie, Pierre D. (1902) *Walkyries, Swan-Maidens, Norns: The Religion of the Teutons.* Dallas: Ginn & Co.

Clover, C. (1986) Maiden Warriors and Other Sons. *Journal of English and Germanic Philology.* (1) 85, 35-49.

Cook, A.S. (1889) *Judith, an old English epic fragment.* Boston: Heath

Crossley-Holland, K. (1980) *The Norse Myths.* London: Penguin

Crossley- Holland, K. (1999) *Beowulf* Oxford: Oxford University Press

Damico, H. (1984) *Beowulf's Weahltheow and the Valkyrie Tradition.* Madison: University of Wisconsin Press.

Driscoll, M.J. (2008) *Ágrip* London: Viking Society for Northern Research

Ellis Davidson H. and Fisher P. (2008). *Saxo Grammaticus. The History of the Danes. Books I–IX.* Woodbridge: D.S Brewer.

Ellis H. R. 1943. *The Road to Hel: A Study in the Conception of the Dead in Old Norse Literature.* Cambridge University Press.

Ellis-Davidson H. (1971) *The Battle God of the Vikings –* Garmondsway Lecture. York: University of York

Ellis-Davidson, H. (1964) *Gods and Myths of Northern Europe.* London: Penguin

Ellis-Davidson, H. (1998) *Roles of the Northern Goddess* London: Routledge

Estés, C.P. (1992) *Women who run with wolves.* London: Rider

Evans, L. (2003) *The Anglo-Saxon / Viking Weaving Sword.* London: Lanista

Ewing, T. (2008) *Gods and Worshippers in the Viking and Germanic world.* Stroud: Tempus

Finch, R.G. (1965) *The Saga of the Volsungs* London: Nelson

Fisher, P. (1979) *History of the Danes.* Totowa NJ, USA: Rowman and Littlefield.

Flom, G.T. (1937) *The old Norwegian general law of the Gulathing [Gulathingslög] according to codex Gl. k. S. 1154 folio.* Urbana: University of Illinois at Urbana

Griffiths, B. (1996) *Aspects of Anglo Saxon Magic.* Hockwold-cum-Wilton: Anglo Saxon Books.

Grimm, Jacob. *Teutonic Mythology.* 4 vols. New York: Dover.

Guerber, H.A. (1914) *Myths of the Norsemen.* London: George Harrap

Halldorsson, O. (2000) *Danish Kings and the Jomsvikings in the greatest saga of Olaf Tryggvason.* London: Viking Society for Northern Research

Hammond, B. (2013) *British Artefacts Volumes 1-3.* Witham: Greenlight

Hatto, A.T. (1964) *The Nibelungenlied* London: Penguin Classics

Heinrich, B. (1999) *Mind of the Raven: Investigations and Adventures with Wolf-Birds* London: Harper Collins

Herbert, K. (1994) *Looking for the Lost Gods of England.* Pinner: Anglo Saxon Books

Hight, G.A. (1972) *The Saga of Grettir the Strong.* London: Dent

Hollander L. (1962) *The Poetic Edda.* Texas: University of Texas Press.

Hollander, L. (1967) The Saga of the Ynglings. USA: University of Texas Press

Hollander, L (1980). *Old Norse Poems: The Most Important Non-skaldic Verse Not Included in the Poetic Edda. London:* Forgotten Books.

Hollander, L. (!998) *Njal's Saga.* Ware: Wordsworth Classics

Hreinssen, V. (Ed.) (2000) *The Sagas of the Icelanders.* London: Allen Lane/ Penguin

Jennings, P. (2007) *Heathen Paths: Viking & Anglo Saxon Heathen Beliefs.* Milverton: Capall Bann

Jennings, P. (2013) *The Wild Hunt and its followers.* Halstead: Gruff

Jesch J. (1991). *Women in the Viking Age.* Woodbridge: Boydell.

Jochens J. (1996). *Old Norse Images of Women*. Philadelphia: University of Pennsylvania

Jochens, Jenny M. "The Medieval Icelandic Heroine: Fact or Fiction?" *Viator* 17 (1986): 35-50.

Jones, G. (1988) *Eirik the Red and other Icelandic sagas*. Oxford: Oxford University Press

Kershaw, N. (1922) *Anglo Saxon and Norse Poems*. Cambridge: Cambridge University Press

Kristin, G. (1997) *Óðsmál* Reykjavik: Freyjukettir

Leszek Gardeła (2013) 'Warrior-women' in Viking Age Scandinavia? A preliminary archaeological study *Analecta Archaeologica Ressoviensia* 8 (1) 273-339

Macleod, M & Mees ,B. (2006) *Runic Amulets and Magic Objects*. Woodbridge: Boydell

Magnusson & Palsson (1976) *Laxdæla Saga*. Harmondsworth: Penguin

Magnusson, M. (1987) *Iceland Saga* London: Bodley Head

McGrath, S. (1997) *Asyniur: Women's Mysteries in the Northern Tradition*. Milverton: Capall Bann.

McKinnell, J. (1987) *Viga-Glums Saga*. London: Canongate

Mortimer, P. (2011) *Woden's Warriors*. Little Downham: Anglo Saxon Books

Nasstrom, B.M. (1995) *Freyja - the Great Goddess of the North*. Lund Studies in History of Religions 5. University of Lund: Lund, Sweden.

Nelson, N.F. (1962) *The Saga of the Jomsvikings*. London: Thomas Nelson

North, R. (1997) *Heathen Gods in Old English Literature*. Cambridge: Cambridge University Press

North & Allard Eds. (2007) *Beowulf & Other Stories: a new introduction to Old English, Old Icelandic and Anglo Norman literatures.* Harlow: Pearson Education

Owen, G.R. (1985) *Rites and religions of the Anglo Saxons.* Dorset: Dorset Press

Pálsson, H & Edwards, P (1969). *Eyrbyggja saga* London: Penguin

Pálsson, H & Edwards, P (1978) *Orkneyinga Saga* London: Penguin

Paxon, Diana L. (2006) *Essential Asatru: walking the path of Norse Paganism.* USA: Citadel

Pollington, S. (1989) *The Warriors Way – England in the Viking Age.* London: Blandford

Pollington, S. (1996) *The English Warrior from earliest times till 1066.* Hockwold-cum-Wilton: Anglo Saxon Books

Pollington, S. (2011) *The Elder Gods.* Little Downham: Anglo Saxon Press.

Purser, P. (2013) *Her Syndan Wælcyrian: Illuminating the Form and Function of the Valkyrie-Figure in the Literature,Mythology, and Social Consciousness of Anglo-Saxon England.* USA: Georgia State University http://scholarworks.gsu.edu/english_diss/104

Saxo Grammaticus Gesta Danorum Book 3. in Fisher (1979) *History of the Danes.* Totowa NJ: Rowman and Littlefield.

Simek, R. (1993) *Dictionary of Northern Mythology* (Trans. A Hall) Woodbridge: DS Brewer

Strand, B. (1981) "Women in Gesta Danorum." *Saxo Grammaticus: A Medieval Author Between Norse and Latin Culture.* Copenhagen: Museum Tusculanum Press.

Sturlusson, S. (1931) *Heimskringla* (Ed. Monsen & Smith) London: Heffer

Sturlusson, S. (1954) *The Prose Edda* (trans. J Young) USA: University of California Press

Tacitus (98CE) *Germania.* (Trans. A Hamilton) Penguin: London

Tolkien, C. (1960) *The Saga of King Heidrik the Wise.* London: T Nelson & Sons.

Tolley, C. (2008) *Grottasǫngr.* London: Viking Society for Northern Research

Various (2011) *Longman Anthology of Old English, Old Icelandic, and Anglo-Norman Literatures* (Ed. by North, Allard, Gillies) London: Routledge

About the Author

Pete Jennings was born in Ipswich, Suffolk in 1953, and has had careers as a telephone engineer, sales manager and more latterly as a registered and qualified social worker. He is also a registered and qualified counsellor & psychotherapist. He now lives on the Essex / Suffolk border.

Outside of his main working life he has sung with rock and folk bands, been a disco dj and radio presenter, Anglo Saxon & Viking re-enactor, actor & Pagan activist. He has had over a dozen books published and regularly lectures in the UK and abroad. He has a low boredom threshold, likes dogs, 70s prog rock, books, real ale and his wife Sue, but not necessarily in that order.

Books & e Books by Pete Jennings

Pathworking (with Pete Sawyer) – Capall Bann (1993)
Northern Tradition Information Pack – Pagan Federation (1996)
Supernatural Ipswich – Gruff (1997)
Pagan Paths – Rider (2002)
The Northern Tradition – Capall Bann (2003)
Mysterious Ipswich – Gruff (2003)
Old Glory & the Cutty Wren – Gruff (2003)
Pagan Humour – Gruff (2005)
The Gothi & the Rune Stave – Gruff (2005)
Haunted Suffolk – Tempus (2006)
Tales & Tours – Gruff (2006)
Heathen Paths: Viking and Anglo Saxon Pagan Beliefs – Capall Bann (2007)
Haunted Ipswich – Tempus/ History Press (2010)
Penda: Heathen King of Mercia and his Anglo Saxon World. – Gruff (2013)
The Wild Hunt & its followers – Gruff (2013)
Blacksmith Gods, Myths, Magicians & Folklore – Moon Books/ Pagan Portals (2014)
Confidently Confused – Gruff (2014)
Adventures in Ælphame – Gruff (2015)
Valkyries, selectors of heroes: their roles within Viking & Anglo Saxon Heathen beliefs. – Gruff (2016)

Pete Jennings has also contributed with others to:
Modern Pagans: an investigation of contemporary Pagan practices. (Eds. V Vale & J.Sulak.) San Francisco: RE/Search (2001)
The Museum of Witchcraft: a Magical History – (Ed. Kerriann Godwin) Boscastle: Occult Art Co. (2011)
Heathen Information Pack – UK: Pagan Federation (2014)
The Call of the God: an anthology exploring the divine masculine within modern Paganism (Ed. Frances Billinghurst) Australia: TDM (2015)

Details of how to obtain Pete Jennings' books and an up to date diary of lectures by Pete Jennings can be found at www.gippeswic.demon.co.uk.

Some books are also available as electronic digital versions via

www.amazon.co.uk/Pete-Jennings/e/B0034OPQP8

Pete regularly writes shorter magazine articles and reviews, especially for Wiðowinde & Pagan Dawn. He was also the editor of the Gippeswic magazine. You can also follow Pete Jennings and Ealdfaeder Anglo Saxons on Facebook.

For appearances of Pete with his Ealdfaeder Anglo Saxons re-enactor friends go to www.ealdfaeder.org

References

[1] Bellows, A. (1936) *The Poetic Edda* www.sacred-texts.com Accessed 1/12/15

[2] Nafnaþulur is a part of the *Skáldskaparmál* in the Prose Edda.

[3] Mortimer, P. (2011) *Woden's Warriors.* Little Downham: Anglo Saxon Books p.213

[4] Hollander, L. (1962) *The Poetic Edda.* Austin: University of Texas Press.

[5] Grimm, Jacob (1882) *Teutonic Mythology Volume I.* trans. Stallybrass. London: George Bell and Sons.

[6] Macleod, M & Mees ,B. (2006) *Runic Amulets and Magic Objects.* Woodbridge: Boydell

[7] Crossley- Holland, K. (1999) *Beowulf* Oxford: Oxford University Press

[8] Ellis-Davidson, H. (1964) *Gods and Myths of Northern Europe.* London: Penguin

[9] Gesta Hammaburgensis ecclesiae pontificum ('Deeds of the Bishops of Hamburg') written between 1073 and 1076 by Adam of Bremen.

[10] *History of the Archbishops of Hamburg-Bremen* by Adam of Bremen was written in the 11th century quoted in Bauschatz, P. (1982) *The Well and the Tree: World and Time in Early Germanic Culture* USA: University of Massachusetts Press

[11] Pollington, S. (2011) *The Elder Gods.* Little Downham: Anglo Saxon Books p313

[12] Anon. (1991) *Beowulf* (trans. J Porter) Little Downham: Anglo Saxon Books

[13] Pollington, S. (2011) *The Elder Gods.* Little Downham: Anglo Saxon Books p328

[14] Simek, R. (1993) *Dictionary of Northern Mythology* (Trans. A Hall) DS Brewer: Woodbridge.

[15] Skaldi has Thrymheim, Heimdall Himinbjorg, Thor's hall is Thrudheim, Frigga has Fensalir, Ullr's hall is Ydalir, Forseti rules Glitnir, Balder (before his death) has Breidablik. Viđi is the home of Viđarr and Saga tells her tales in Sokkvabekk. Additionally there are two general temple halls: Gladsheim for gods and Vingolfhal for goddesses. Of course Freyja takes half of the valiant slain to her hall Sessrunnr where their familes also enter.

[16] Bellows, H. (1936) *The Poetic Edda.* www.sacred-texts.com accessed 5/11/15

[17] Viđarr and Vali, the sons of Odin; Modi and Magni, the sons of Thor, Balder & Hođr plus two humans Lif and Lifthrasir. Also probably most of the goddesses because no story is told of their destruction.

[18] Grímnismál is part of the Poetic Edda (Hollander, 1962) It is preserved in the Codex Regius manuscript and also the AM 748 I 4 fragment of Icelandic vellum parchment.

[19] Saxo Grammaticus *Gesta Danorum Book 3.* in Fisher (1979) *History of the Danes.* Totowa NJ: Rowman and Littlefield.

[20] Ellis-Davidson, H. (1964) *Gods and Myths of Northern Europe.* London: Penguin p184-185

[21] Jennings, P. (2013) *The Wild Hunt and its followers.* Gruff: Halstead

[22] Kershaw, N. (1922) *Anglo Saxon and Norse Poems.* Cambridge. p117

[23] Nasstrom, B.M. (1995) *Freyja - the Great Goddess of the North.* Lund Studies in

History of Religions 5. University of Lund: Lund, Sweden.
[24] Cathedral of St. Peter at Schleswig.
[25] http://www.patheos.com/blogs/pantheon/2011/01/wyrd-designs-correcting-common-misperceptions-freyja-the-valkyrie/ Accessed 27/11/15
[26] Simek, R. (1993) *Dictionary of Northern Mythology (Trans. A Hall)* DS Brewer: Woodbridge.
[27] Grímnismál 23.
[28] Jennings, P. (2013) *The Wild Hunt and its followers*. Gruff: Halstead
[29] Westcoat, E. (2015) Valknut: The heart of the slain? *Óðrœrir* 1 (3)
[30] Paxon, Diana L. (2006) *Essential Asatru: walking the path of Norse Paganism.* USA: Citadel Press p138-139
[31] Pálsson, H & Edwards, P (1969). *Eyrbyggja saga* London: Penguin
[32] Herjan =Leader of Hosts i.e. Odin / Woden
[33] Jesch J. (1991) *Women in the Viking Age*. Woodbridge: Boydell. p154 (occurs in Skáldskaparmál)
[34] Pollington, S. (1996) *The English Warrior from earliest times till 1066.* Hockwold-cum-Wilton: Anglo Saxon Books p49
[35] Tacitus, *Germania*
[36] Saga of Eirik the Red
[37] Clover, C. (1986) Maiden Warriors and Other Sons *Journal of English and Germanic Philology* , (1) 85, 35-49.
[38] Saxo Grammaticus. *Gesta Danorum* in Fisher (1979) *History of the Danes.* Totowa NJ: Rowman and Littlefield.
[39] Jochens, Jenny M. "The Medieval Icelandic Heroine: Fact or Fiction?" Viator 17 (1986): 35-50.
[40] Jennings, P. (2007*) Heathen Paths: Viking & Anglo Saxon Heathen Beliefs*. Milverton: Capall Bann
[41] Jesch, J.(1991) *Women of the Viking Age.* Woodbridge: Boydell
[42] Hulda quoted in http://blogs.transparent.com/icelandic/2012/10/03/the-mystery-of-shieldmaidens/ Accessed 24/11/15
[43] Regal, M. S. (2000) Gisli Sursson's Saga IN Hreinssen, V. (Ed.) (2000) *The Sagas of the Icelanders.* London: Allen Lane/ Penguin   p. 496–557.
[44] Magnusson & Palsson (1976) *Laxdæla Saga*. Harmondsworth: Penguin p125-128
[45] Cook, A.S. (1889) *Judith, an old English epic fragment.* Boston: Heath
[46] *Judith* is found in the same manuscript as *Beowulf*, the *Nowell Codex* (London, British Library, Cotton MS Vitellius A. XV), dated ca. 975-1025
[47] Evans, L. (2003) *The Anglo-Saxon / Viking Weaving Sword*. London: Lanista
[48] http://nms.scran.ac.uk/database/record.php?usi=000-000-099-748-C Accessed 12/11/15
[49] Ballard, S. (2007) 15. Stirring Women, Weapons and Weaving: Aspects of gender identity and symbols of power in early Anglo Saxon England. In Hamilton,

Whitehouse & Wright (Eds.) *The Archaeology of Women*. Walnut Creek CA: Left Coast Press

[50] Gardela, L. (2003) Warrior-women' in Viking Age Scandinavia? A preliminary archaeological study, Analecta *Archaeologica Ressoviensia* 8 (1) 273-339

[51] Anon. (1996) *The Poetic Edda*. (trans C. Larrington,) Oxford: Oxford University Press

[52] Burfield, B. (2014) Odin: warrior god. *In Wiđowinde* 1 (171), p31-34

[53] Sturlusson, S. (1931) *Heimskringla* (Ed. Monsen & Smith) London: Heffer

[54] Flom, G.T. (1937) *The old Norwegian general law of the Gulathing [Gulathingslög] according to codex Gl. k. S. 1154 folio*. Urbana: University of Illinois at Urbana

[55] Owen, G.R. (1985) *Rites and religions of the Anglo Saxons*. Dorset: Dorset Press p28-29

[56] Jesch J. (1991). *Women in the Viking Age*. Woodbridge: Boydell. p142-143

[57] Aswynn, F. (1990) *Leaves of Yggdrasil*. USA: Llewellyn p233-234.

[58] Sturlusson, S. (1954) *The Prose Edda* (trans. J Young) USA: University of California Press

[59] Hollander, L (1980). *Old Norse Poems: The Most Important Non-skaldic Verse Not Included in the Poetic Edda*. London: Forgotten Books.

[60] https://www.newscientist.com/article/dn17556-crows-use-multitools-but-do-they-plan-ahead/ Accessed 6/12/15

[61] http://sploid.gizmodo.com/watch-a-genius-crow-solve-8-complex-puzzles-in-perfect-1520343494 Accessed 6/12/15

[62] http://www.bbc.co.uk/news/magazine-31604026 Accessed 6/12/15

[63] Scientific investigation has revealed evidence of regional dialects and specific sounds associated with particular individuals. They also use beaks and wings to make gestures. http://www.livescience.com/17213-ravens-gestures-animal-communication.html Accessed 6/12/15

[64] Heinrich, B. (1999) *Mind of the Raven: Investigations and Adventures with Wolf-Birds* London: Harper Collins

[65] http://www.cracked.com/article_19042_6-terrifying-ways-crows-are-way-smarter-than-you-think.html

[66] Pálsson & Edwards (1978) *Orkneyinga Saga*. London: Penguin

[67] Sturlusson, S. 1931) *Heimskringla* (Ed. Monsen & Smith) London: Heffer

[68] Ellis-Davidson, H. (1998) *Roles of the Northern Goddess* London: Routledge p45

[69] Hollander, L. (2010) *Old Norse Poems*. London: Abela p109-122

[70] Fagrskinna so called from the 'Fair Leather' form of the original document burnt but previously copied onto vellum. It draws upon other written sources and in turn informs Heimskringla.

[71] Hollander, L. (2010) *Old Norse Poems*. London: Abela p129-139

[72] Hatto, A.T. (1964) *The Nibelungenlied* London: Penguin Classics

[73] Purser, P. (2013) http://scholarworks.gsu.edu/english_diss/104   Accessed 27/11/15

[74] *Sermo Lupi ad Anglos, quando Dani maxime persecuti sunt eos quod fuit anno millesimo XIIII ab incarnatione domini nostri Iesu Cristi*

[75] Ewing, T. (2008) *Gods and Worshippers in the Viking and Germanic world.* Stroud: Tempus

[76] *De laudis virginitatis* (Oxford, Bodleian library, Digby 146)

[77] *Cotton Cleopatra A. iii*

[78] Herbert, K. (1994) *Looking for the Lost Gods of England.* Pinner: Anglo Saxon Books p21

[79] Tolley, C. (2008) *Grottasǫngr.* London: Viking Society for Northern Research. p. 39

[80] Jesch (1991) *Women of the Viking Age.* Woodbridge: Boydell p184

[81] Byock, J. (1998) *The Saga of King Hrolf Kraki* London: Penguin

[82] Hollander, L. (!998) *Njal's Saga.* Ware: Wordsworth Classics

[83] Flat-island book known as GkS 1005 fol. and by the Latin name Codex Flateyensis.
An online English translation can be found at:
http://www.northvegr.org/sagas%20annd%20epics/miscellaneous/the%20flately%20book/

[84] Jones, G. (1988) *Eirik the Red and other Icelandic sagas.* Oxford: Oxford University Press p158-162

[85] Scudder, B. (1997) Egils Saga IN Hreinsson, V (Ed) *Sagas of the Icelanders.* London: Allen Lane & Penguin.

[86] Fox & Palsson (1974) *Grettirs Saga* Canada: University of Toronto Press

[87] Tolkien, C. (1960) *The Saga of King Heidrek the Wise.* London: Thomas Nelson & Sons

[88] Kunz, K. (1997) Saga of the People of Laxardal IN Hreinsson, V (Ed) *Sagas of the Icelanders.* London: Allen Lane & Penguin

[89] Attwood, K. (1997) Saga of Gunnlaug Serpent Tongue IN Hreinsson, V (Ed) *Sagas of the Icelanders.* London: Allen Lane & Penguin

[90] Regal, M. (1997) Gisli Sursson's Saga IN Hreinsson, V (Ed) *Sagas of the Icelanders.* London: Allen Lane & Penguin

[91] Contained within *Heimskringla* by Snorri Sturluson.

[92] Accessed 5/12/15
http://www.northvegr.org/sagas%20annd%20epics/icelandic%20family%20sagas/viga%20glums%20saga/026.html

[93] Hunt-Anschutz, A. (2006) Disir: ancestral Goddesses who fight for their kin? In Pagan Dawn (1) p16-18

[94] Bede (1951) *The Ecclesiastical History of the English Nation.* (Trans. J Stevens) London: JM Dent p90-92

[95] Gunnell, T. (1997) Saga of Hrafnkel Frey's Godi IN Hreinsson, V (Ed) *Sagas of the Icelanders.* London: Allen Lane & Penguin

[96] From the *Poetic Edda*

[97] Finch, R.G. (1965) *The Saga of the Volsungs* London: Nelson
[98] Accessed 11/11/15
http://www.northvegr.org/sagas%20annd%20epics/legendary%20heroic%20and%20imaginative%20sagas/old%20heithinn%20tales%20from%20the%20north/index.html
[99] Halldorsson, O. (2000) *Danish Kings and the Jomsvikings in the greatest saga of Olaf Tryggvason.* London: Viking Society for Northern Research
[100] Bede (1951) *The Ecclesiastical History of the English Nation.* (Trans. J Stevens) London: JM Dent p94
[101] North, R. (1997) *Heathen Gods in Old English Literature.* Cambridge: Cambridge University Press
[102] Ellis- Davidson (1971) *The Battle God of the Vikings* – Garmondsway Lecture. York: University of York
[103] Simek, R. (1993) *Dictionary of Northern Mythology* (Trans. A Hall) DS Brewer: Woodbridge
[104] MacLeod, M. Mees, B (2006). *Runic Amulets and Magic Objects.* Woodbridge: Boydell Press p37
[105] Liestol, A. (1966) The Runes of Bergen: Voices from the Middle Ages. Minnesota Historical Society 1 49-58
[106] Purser, P. (2013) http://scholarworks.gsu.edu/english_diss/104 Accessed 27/11/15
[107] Exeter Cathedral Library MS 3501, also known as the Codex Exoniensis, Dated between 960-990 CE
[108] Rundkvist, M. (2013) Valkyrie Figurine from Hårby, Denmark IN *Wiðowinde* (1) 165 p33
[109] Hammond, B. (2013) *British Artefacts Volume 3- Late Saxon, Late Viking & Norman.* Witham: Greenlight p37 1.1.3-e
[110] Harris, J (2009) The Rök stone through Anglo Saxon Eyes in *Anglo-Saxons and the north*
essays reflecting the theme of the 10th Meeting of the International Society of Anglo-Saxonists in Helsinki, August 2001 (ed by Matti Kilpiö) USA: Arizona Center for Medieval and Renaissance Studies in Tempe, Ariz .
... [et al.]. Arizona Center for Medieval and Renaissance Studies in Tempe, Ariz .
[111] Eliason, S. (2005) Viking Horses in *Viking Heritage* magazine (1) 2 p2-8
[112] Eliason, S. (2005) Viking Horses in *Viking Heritage* magazine (1) 2 p11
[113] Jesch J. 1991. *Women in the Viking Age.* Woodbridge: Boydell. p130
[114] Ellis- Davidson (1971) *The Battle God of the Vikings* – Garmondsway Lecture. York: University of York
[115] Griffiths, B. (1996) *Aspects of Anglo Saxon Magic.* Hockwold-cum-Wilton: Anglo Saxon Books. p34
[116] Becker, A (2006) Fylga and Valkyrie: the warriors companions in life and death IN *Wiðowinde* (1) 141 p22-26
[117] Purser, P. (2013) http://scholarworks.gsu.edu/english_diss/104 Accessed

27/11/15

[118] See http://www.forest.gen.nz/Medieval/articles/Oseberg/textiles/TEXTILE.HTM Accessed 3/12/15.

[119] Paulson, I (2002) *Valkyrie Rising* USA: Harperteen

[120] Clarkson, W. (1998) *The Valkyrie Operation*. London: John Blake

[121] Mark, M., & Pearson, C. S. (2001). *The hero and the outlaw: Building extraordinary brands through the power of archetypes*. New York: McGraw-Hill.

[122] Estés, C.P. (1992) *Women who run with wolves.* London: Rider p26

[123] http://spectrum.ieee.org/automaton/robotics/military-robots/nasa-jsc-unveils-valkyrie-drc-robot Accessed 26/11/15

[124] http://www.cobalt-aircraft.com/co50-valkyrie/ Accessed 26/11/15

[125] http://www.thevalkyrie.com/main.html Accessed 24/11/15

[126] Kristin, G. (1997) *Óðsmál* Reykjavik: Freyjukettir

Made in the USA
Middletown, DE
27 June 2021